Cut-and-Tell
Bible Stories

Cut-and-Tell Bible Stories

Jean Stangl

CONCORDIA PUBLISHING HOUSE • SAINT LOUIS

Contents

New Testament

Introduction

Cut-and-Tell Bible Stories presents a unique technique for telling familiar stories. While telling the story, the storyteller folds a sheet of paper, makes a few quick cuts with scissors, unfolds the paper, and presents the audience with a cutout. Using a visual aid in the presence of children helps capture their attention, maintain interest, create an exciting storytelling environment, and stimulate the imagination. Comprehension and retention skills also are fostered through this method.

For each story from the Old and New Testament, you'll find patterns and directions for creating a cutout. Most of the stories require only an 8½ × 11 sheet of paper and scissors. Any additional materials or preparation activities are listed at the beginning of each story. You can use any type of paper; however, construction paper provides more body for the free-standing cutouts.

To prepare, use pencil or chalk to lightly trace the pattern onto a folded sheet of paper. As an option, you could indicate only the numbers and cut in a dot-to-dot fashion. Or, after studying the pattern, you may be able to use it as a guide to free cut your own design. After preparing the sheet of paper, read the story several times, even if it is familiar. Finally, before speaking to the children, make a sample cutting as you practice telling the story.

This innovative method of presenting favorite Bible stories will fascinate preschool through second-grade children. Older children will enjoy making their own cutouts or making a cutout while telling a story to younger children.

Happy storytelling!

Old Testament

Six Special Days

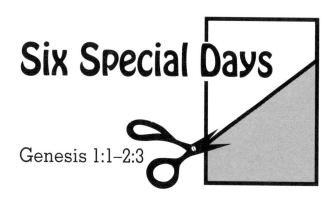

Genesis 1:1–2:3

Materials: One 8½ × 11 sheet of white paper, scissors, crayons
Preparation: Color section A = green, section B = yellow, and section C = a color of your choice. For folding and cutting directions, see the pattern on page 12.

Once, long ago, there was nothing. Only God was here. *(Fold paper lengthwise.)*

Everything was dark. Close your eyes and see how dark it was. God created the light. Open your eyes. See the light? God called the light *day.* The dark He called *night.* Now there would be night and day. There was also an evening and a morning. This was the first day God made.

On the second day, God put space between the waters. He made sure there was some water above the earth. It's stored in clouds. He put air between the water below and the sky above. *(Cut 1 to 2.)* Breathe God's air. *(Ask children to inhale deeply, then exhale.)* There was another evening and morning—the second day.

On the third day, God put all the water on earth in one place. He created dry ground. God called the dry ground *land,* and the waters He called *seas.* God created all the water in the oceans, lakes, and rivers. The oceans hold most of the water on earth because God planned it that way. The water surrounded the dry ground. *(Cut 2 to 3.)*

Grass, flowers, and all kinds of plants grew on the land. There were many trees. *(Slowly cut 3 to 4. Then cut to the unfolded edge of the paper. Unfold the paper.)* Some were big trees with lots of leaves that make shade for us on a hot day. God created some trees to give us fruit to eat. He made apple, peach, and orange trees. Each fruit had its own special seed. God created plants to bloom and to produce seeds so they could keep growing new plants. *(Refold.)*

On the fourth day *(cut 4 to 5),* God created two great lights. *(Cut 5 to 6.)* He put the bright, warm sun in the sky for a light during the day. The sun would be the biggest, brightest light. *(Cut 6 to 7.)* He put the moon in the sky to give a little light at night. Sometimes we see a big, round moon. Other times we see only part of the moon. *(Cut 7 to 8.)* God also made *(cut 8 to 9)* many, many stars. *(Cut 9 to 10. Then cut to the unfolded edge of the paper. Unfold the paper.)* God filled the sky with stars. There are so many that we could never count them. Only God knows how many there are. God's lights are also signs for us. They help us to know the days, months, years, and seasons. God's lights will shine on and on, they will never go out. The sun and the moon will never fall to earth because God keeps them in their special place.

On the fifth day *(refold),* God created all the animals that live in the sea—the giant whales, the red lobsters, and the tiny fish. *(Cut 10 to 11.)* He made everything that lives in the water. *(Cut 11 to 12).* He also created many colorful birds that fly above the earth. *(Cut 12 to 13.)* God made the tiny hummingbirds, the white doves, and the black ravens.

On the sixth day, God created all the animals that live on the land—tigers, elephants, bears, and many more. *(Cut 13 to 14.)* God knew that some animals would be good for carrying things, like horses, and some animals would make good pets, like dogs and cats. The last thing God created was a person. *(Cut 14 to 15.)* He made a *(unfold)* man. God called the man *Adam.*

Then God created a woman so Adam would not be alone. The woman would be his wife. Adam called his wife *Eve.* God put Adam and Eve in charge of His earth.

God looked around His beautiful world. He saw the lights in the sky, the fish in the sea, and the flowers and trees growing. He looked at all the animals He had created. God said that everything He had made was good. Then God looked at the man and woman He had made. God said they were very good. God had finished creating the heavens and the earth. They were just the way God wanted them to be. By the seventh day, God had finished all His work. He rested. God created our wonderful world and everything in it in just six days.

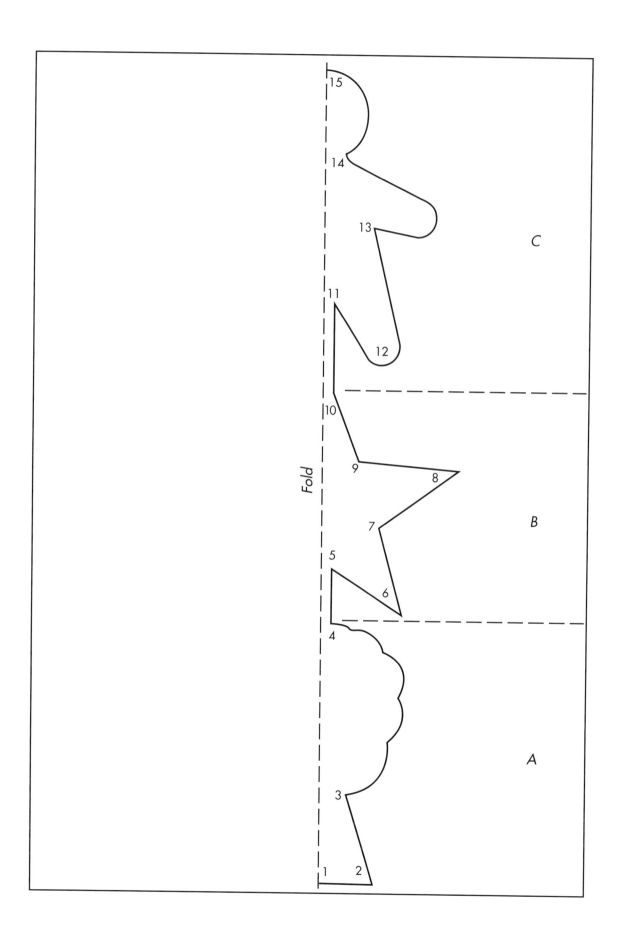

Fold

15

14

13

11

12

10

9

8

7

5

6

4

3

1   2

C

B

A

12

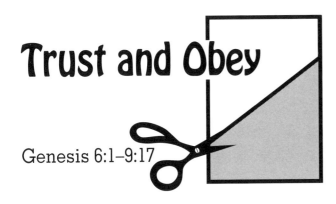

Trust and Obey

Genesis 6:1–9:17

Materials: One 8½ × 11 sheet of light blue paper, scissors
Preparation: None.
For folding and cutting directions, see the pattern on page 15.

Many years after God created it, God looked around His world. It was beautiful. Then God looked at the people living on the earth. He saw that they were full of sin. The people disobeyed Him and did things that they shouldn't. *(Fold line 1.)*

God was very sad. "I will destroy the people whom I have created and all the animals too. I will destroy everything that crawls on the earth and flies in the air," He said. *(Fold line 2.)*

A man named Noah lived on the earth. Noah loved God and did what God wanted him to do. Noah and his wife had three sons. Their names were Shem, Ham, and Japheth. Each son had a wife, but they had no children. Noah and his family trusted and obeyed God.

God told Noah that He was going to destroy all living things on the earth. "I want you to build an ark," God said to Noah. *(Cut 1 to 2.)* "You and your family and pairs of all the animals will live in the ark. Then I will send a great flood that will destroy everything on the earth. You, your family, and the animals will be the only ones I will save." *(Cut 2 to 3.)*

God told Noah exactly how to make the ark. God said the ark should be 450 feet long, 75 feet wide, and 45 feet high. It should have three levels divided into many rooms. Noah should make an opening around the top, a door on one side, and a roof to cover the ark. *(Cut 3 to 4.)* God said the ark should be made of gopher wood. That's what Noah and his sons—Shem, Ham, and Japheth—used to build the ark. *(Cut 4 to 5.)*

As Noah and his sons worked, the people stopped by to watch. They asked Noah what he was doing. When Noah told the people about the flood God would send, they laughed and did not believe him. But Noah trusted God, and he and his sons kept building the ark. *(Cut 5 to 6.)* When the ark was finished, Noah and his sons sealed the entire ark with pitch, or tar. This would keep the giant ship from leaking. God designed the boat to float on the water and to keep everything inside safe and dry. *(Cut 6 to 7.)*

After Noah and his sons finished the ark, God said, "Take your wife, your sons and their wives, and pairs of every living thing, male and female, into the ark. Take animals, birds, and things that creep on the earth. Store food in the ark for you and your family and take hay and wheat and every kind of food that the animals will eat." *(Cut line A.)*

Noah and his wife and Noah's sons and their wives filled the ark with food. They found places for all the animals God brought to the ark. *(Cut line B.)* Now everyone was safe inside. *(Unfold ark. Separate the sections so the ark stands.)* The ark was three stories high. *(Count the stories.)* It had a door. *(Fold down the door to form a ramp.)* And it had an opening at the top—just as God had planned. *(Fold up the top opening.)*

God closed the door of the ark. *(Close the door.)* The rain began to fall. It rained and rained. The water lifted the ark off the ground and carried it away. The sturdy ark floated. *(Move the ark in a rocking motion.)*

It rained for forty days and forty nights. It was a terrible flood. There had never been a flood like it. The flood destroyed every living thing. *(Move the ark in a rocking motion.)* Because God loved Noah, God kept Noah and his family and the animals safe in the ark.

When the flood was over, Noah opened the door of the ark. *(Bend the door down.)* The animals went down the ramp. Then Noah and his family walked out of the ark. Everyone was safe—just as God had promised.

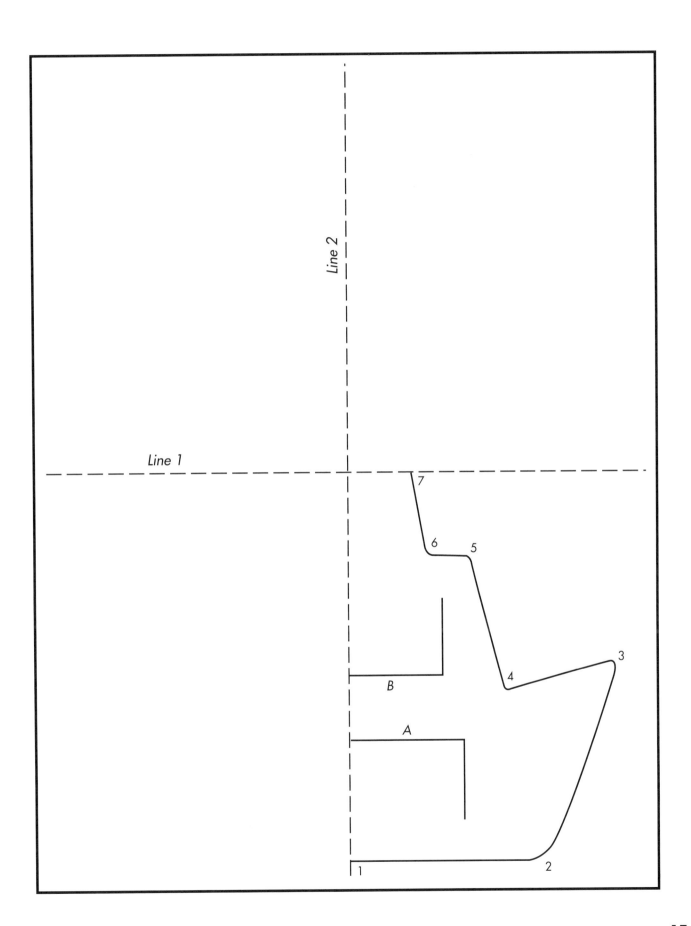

Noah's Helper

Genesis 6:1–8:19

Materials: One 8½ × 11 sheet of white paper, a small scrap of green paper, scissors
Preparation: None.
For folding and cutting directions, see the pattern on page 18.

Noah and his family lived on God's earth. They loved God and obeyed His rules. One day God told Noah that He was going to send a big rain, more rain than anyone had ever seen. *(Fold paper in half.)* God said the rain would flood the earth. It would destroy all the people and all the animals. But God loved Noah. He told Noah to build an ark. God would use the ark to keep Noah and his family safe during the flood. *(Cut 1 to 2.)*

Noah and his three sons built the ark just the way God told them. It was hard work, and it took them a long time. When they finished, Noah and his family put pairs of every kind of animal inside—a male and a female. They put big animals, little animals, and every animal that crawled on the ground inside the ark. Noah and his sons gathered wheat and hay and other food for the animals. They also took food for the family to eat. Finally, everything they needed was inside the ark. Noah had done everything that God had told him to do. Then Noah and his wife and his sons and their wives went inside the ark. God closed the door. *(Cut 2 to 3.)* God told Noah that in seven days it would begin to rain, and it did.

The rain poured down from the sky. *(Cut 3 to 4.)* Harder and harder the rains came. So much rain fell that the water lifted the ark up, up, above the earth. *(Cut 4 to 5.)*

The rain kept falling. The hills, rocks, and mountains were covered with water. All the trees were covered with water. Soon everything in God's world was under the water. *(Cut 5 to 6.)* But God kept Noah and his family and the animals safe. They floated around in the ark on top of the water. *(Cut 6 to 7.)*

It rained for forty days and forty nights. Noah and his family waited and waited. They ate and slept on the ark. They fed the animals and watched over them. But water still covered everything. Had God forgotten about them? Noah and his family kept waiting.

God had not forgotten about Noah. After 150 days, He made the wind blow over the water, and the water started to disappear. Some soaked into the ground. The rest of the water filled the lakes, the rivers, and the oceans. *(Cut 7 to 8.)*

Soon, the ark came to rest on a mountain. *(Cut 8 to 9.)* Noah opened a window and looked out. He saw that the waters were going down, down. *(Cut 9 to 10.)* But the water still covered almost everything. At the end of forty days, Noah opened the window again. He took a raven from its cage and sent it off through the window. The raven could not find a place to land so it flew around and around. Then Noah sent a *(unfold)* dove out the window. It flew off *(fly dove in circles),* but it soon returned to the ark because it couldn't find a place to land. Water was everywhere.

Noah waited seven days *(count one to seven),* a week, and he sent the dove out again. The dove returned, but this time in its mouth was *(place green paper so it extends beyond the beak)* a leaf from an olive tree.

The water was disappearing. *(Remove leaf.)* Noah waited seven more days *(count one to seven)*, another week, and sent the dove out for the third time. It flew away and never came back. *(Fly dove behind you.)*

Noah knew that the rains and the great flood were over. He and his family and all the animals walked out of the ark onto dry ground, just the way God had planned it. Noah and his family were happy that God kept His promise to keep them safe. They thanked God for taking care of them. *(Fly dove back.)* The dove was Noah's helper because God used it to show Noah when it was safe to leave the ark.

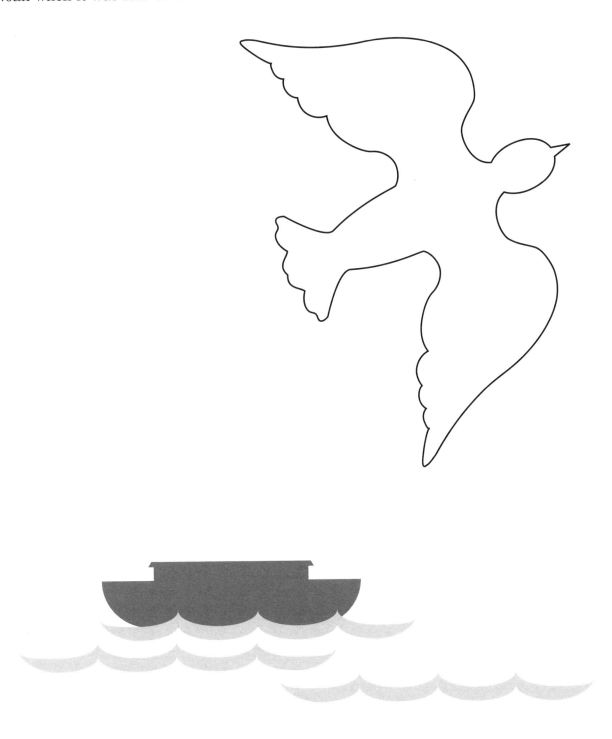

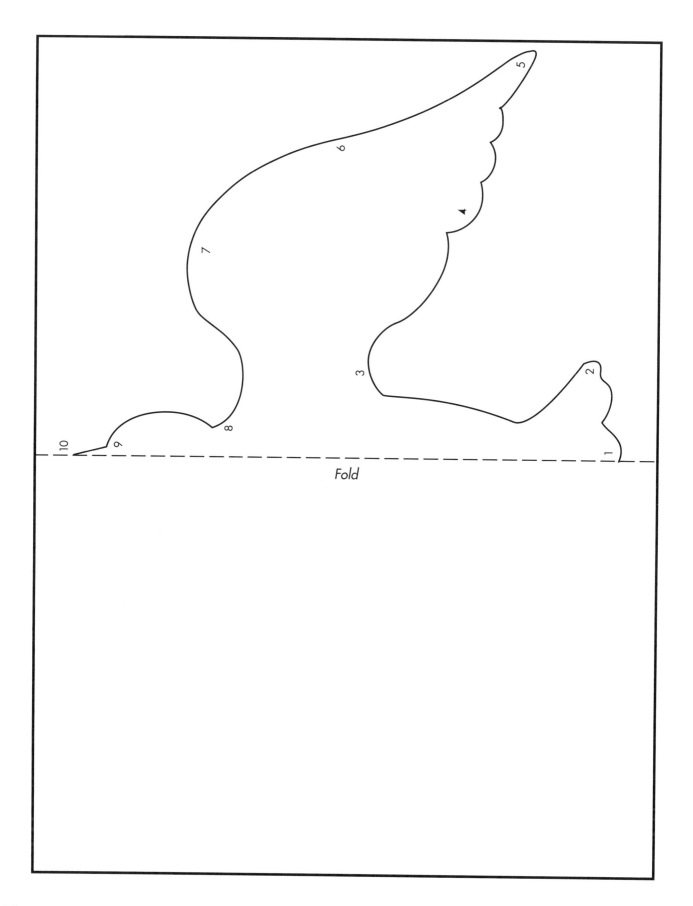

Fold

18

Joseph Feeds His Family

Genesis 37:1–36; 39:1–45:28

Materials: One 8½ × 11 sheet of paper, crayons, scissors
Preparation: Using several different crayons, completely color one side of the paper.
For folding and cutting directions, see the pattern on page 21.

Joseph was the eleventh son of a man named Jacob. Joseph knew that his father loved him very much. Jacob had even given Joseph a beautiful coat with long sleeves to show how much he loved him. Joseph liked the coat, but it made his brothers angry and jealous. *(Fold on line A with colorful side showing.)*

His brothers seemed to get more angry when Joseph told them about a dream he had. "In my dream you were all bowing down to me," he said. The brothers didn't like the idea that Joseph would rule over them.

One day, Jacob sent Joseph to check on his brothers, who were watching the sheep in a distant field. When Joseph got there, his brothers weren't happy to see him. In fact, they grabbed him, tore off his beautiful coat, and threw him in a deep hole. *(Fold on line B.)*

"Let's kill him!" Joseph heard his brothers say.

"No," said Reuben, Joseph's oldest brother. "I don't want him to die."

Instead of letting Joseph go, his brothers sold him to a group of traders traveling to Egypt. *(Cut 1 to 2.)* The traders sold Joseph as a slave to Potiphar. Even though Joseph was in Egypt and far away from his family, he knew God would take care of him. *(Cut 2 to 3.)* Joseph worked hard for Potiphar, but Potiphar's wife accused Joseph of a crime. Potiphar sent Joseph to jail.

But God was with Joseph, even in jail. When Pharaoh had a dream, God let Joseph know the dream meant there would be seven years when the farmers would grow lots of grain. Then after those seven years, there would be seven years when the farmers wouldn't be able to grow any grain. Joseph knew God wanted him to tell Pharaoh to store the grain from the seven good years so the people would have enough to eat when the famine came. *(Cut 3 to 4.)*

Pharaoh thought Joseph had a good plan. He put Joseph in charge of gathering and handing out the grain. Joseph stored the grain during the seven good years. Then he sold grain to the people during the seven bad years. God blessed Joseph and made him a powerful man in Egypt.

One day, ten brothers came to buy grain from Joseph. They bowed down before him because he was an important man. Joseph realized that the men were his brothers, the ones who had sold him into slavery! *(Cut 4 to 5.)* The brothers did not recognize Joseph, though. He was dressed in expensive clothes and had chains of gold around his neck and rings with precious stones on his fingers.

Joseph spoke roughly to his brothers. "What are you doing here, and where do you come from?"

"We are from Canaan. We have come to buy food," answered one of the brothers.

"You are spies," Joseph replied. "You have come to see the damage from the famine and to see if we have any grain." *(Cut 5 to 6.)*

"Oh, no, my lord," said another brother. "We are your servants, and we've come to buy food. We are all brothers. Our youngest brother is at home with our father, and another brother is no more. We are not spies."

"You will have to prove it," said Joseph. "I will keep one of you here. The rest of you will go home and bring your youngest brother back with you."

Joseph pointed to one of the brothers and told a servant to put him in prison. Then Joseph told his servants to fill sacks with grain. "Go now," he ordered the other brothers. "Take these sacks of grain. But bring back your youngest brother so I will know you are telling the truth." *(Cut 6 to 7.)* The brothers left.

When Joseph's brothers returned to Egypt, they bowed before him again. "This is our youngest brother, Benjamin, and here are some presents sent by our father," they said.

"Set our best table," Joseph ordered his servants. "These men will join me for dinner." *(Don't cut 7 to 8. Cut 8 to 9.)* Joseph looked at the brothers as they ate. He was happy to have them all there.

Before they returned home, Joseph told them, "I am Joseph, your brother, whom you sold into slavery in Egypt." His brothers looked frightened and ashamed. *(Cut 9 to 10.)*

Joseph said quickly, "Don't feel bad anymore. God sent me here to save your lives and the lives of your families. He made me a ruler. He gave me power to understand dreams. And He has given me two sons. Go back home and tell my father. Bring Jacob, your wives and your children, and all that you own. I want you to live here in this land. I will give you food and take care of all of you." And he sent them off with food and wagons so they could bring their families back to Egypt.

Joseph watched them leave. *(Cut 10 to 11, cutting through only one fold.)* He smiled. Joseph had forgiven his brothers long ago, and was happy they were moving to Egypt. He loved his family and wanted them to be near him. Soon, he would get to see his father again! *(Cut 11 to 12, cutting through only one fold.)* Joseph's smile grew even bigger as he remembered how God had been at work in his life. Joseph knew God had used him to do something good. *(Unfold and stand up your coat of many colors.)*

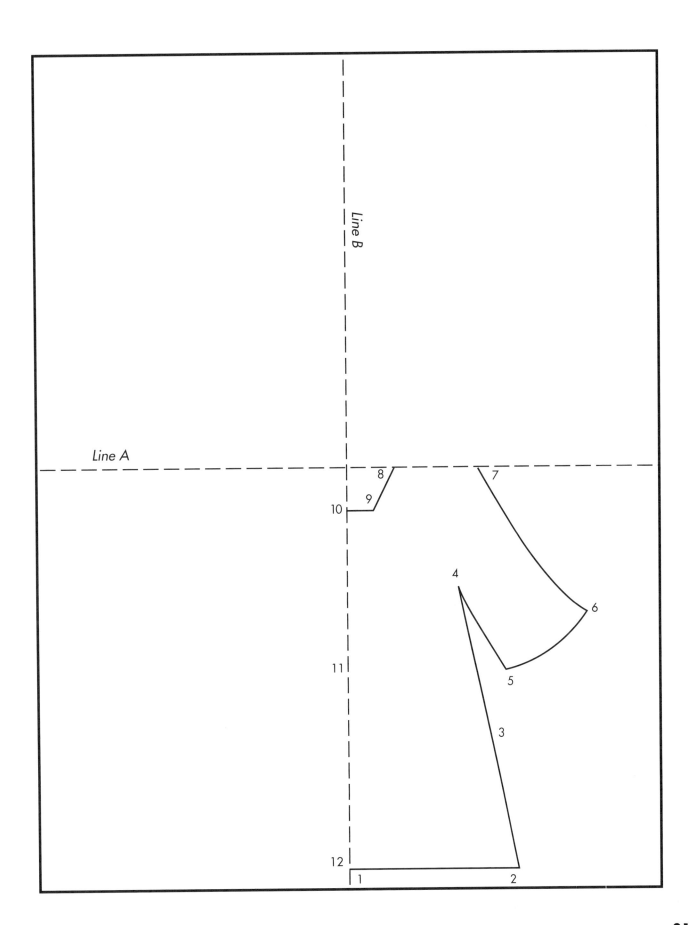

Line B

Line A

A Path through the Sea

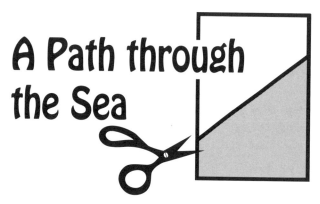

Exodus 3:1–14:31

Materials: One 8½ × 11 sheet of light blue paper, broken red crayon, scissors

Preparation: Remove the paper from the crayon. Lightly color both sides of the paper using the flat side of the crayon.

For folding and cutting directions, see the pattern on page 24.

Moses was taking care of his father-in-law's sheep. As he led them near a mountain, Moses saw something strange. He saw a bush that was on fire, but the bush was not burning up. Moses went to take a closer look, and God spoke to him out of the burning bush. "I want you to take My people and lead them out of Egypt," God said to Moses. "Now they are slaves in Egypt, but I want them to have their own land, the land of Canaan." *(Fold up along line 1.)*

Moses did not want to go. He told God that he would not know what to say to the people and that no one would believe him. God told Moses not to worry. He said "I will be with you and will give you the words to say." God also said that He would send Moses' brother, Aaron, to help him. God promised Moses that He would take care of everything.

Moses did what God asked. He gathered the Israelites together. He told the people about the land that God wanted them to have. "We must get ready to go to Canaan, God's Promised Land," Moses said. *(Fold down along line 2.)*

After they talked to the people, Moses and Aaron went to talk to Pharaoh, the ruler of Egypt. "God says you must let the Israelites go," Moses told Pharaoh. "They should no longer be your slaves." *(Unfold. Hold the two ends of the paper together as you cut, but do not crease the fold.)*

Pharaoh did not want to let the people go. He needed them to work. Because Pharaoh wouldn't let the Israelites go, God brought plagues on the Egyptian people and Pharaoh. There were frogs and flies, sores and hail, locusts, and many more problems. Finally, God sent an angel to kill the oldest boy in every Egyptian family, even the Pharaoh's son died. But God protected the children of the Israelites. The Pharaoh agreed to let the Israelites go. Everyone took their cattle and flocks of sheep and started for the Promised Land.

Once he saw them leaving, however, Pharaoh changed his mind. He still wanted the Israelites to work for him. Pharaoh gathered his army and followed the Israelites so he could bring them back to Egypt. *(Cut 1 to 2.)*

God led His people out of Egypt, through the wilderness, toward the Red Sea. God guided the Israelites during the day from a pillar of cloud. When they traveled at night, God led them from a pillar of fire. *(Cut 2 to 3.)* God told Moses where to camp so Pharaoh would think that the Israelites were lost. *(Cut 3 to 4.)*

Pharaoh and his army caught up with the Israelites as they were camping by the Red Sea. *(Cut 4 to 5.)* The people were afraid when they saw Pharaoh and his men marching toward them. They were angry at Moses. *(Cut 5 to 6.)* "You brought us here to die in the wilderness," they said. *(Cut 6 to 7.)*

"Don't be afraid," Moses answered them. "Stand firm and see how God will save us from the Egyptians. You will never see these Egyptians again. God will fight for you." *(Cut 7 to 8.)* God told Moses to march the Israelites toward the water.

The people moved toward the Red Sea, but the water was too deep for them to cross to the other side. Pharaoh was close behind them. There was no place to go. What would happen now? *(Cut 8 to 9.)*

"Raise your staff and stretch out your hand over the sea to divide the water," God told Moses. *(Cut 9 to 10.)* "You will all walk on dry land. The Egyptians will try to follow you, but don't worry about them." *(Cut 10 to 11.)*

The pillar of cloud that had been leading the Israelites now moved behind them. *(Cut 11 to 12.)* It was dark on Pharaoh's side, but on the side where the Israelites were, it was light. *(Cut 12 to 13.)*

Moses obeyed God and stretched his hand out over the Red Sea. *(Cut to the edge of the paper.)* The Lord made a strong east wind blow across the water. *(Hold the ends of both cut edges and fan them back and forth.)* It divided the water and made a pathway through the sea. The waters stood on both sides like walls. *(Fold up sections B and C so section A forms a path.)* The people walked across the sea to the other side on dry ground.

Pharaoh and his men chased after the Israelites down the dry path. "Stretch your hand over the sea again," God said to Moses. Moses did. The great rushing waters returned and covered the chariots, the horsemen, Pharaoh, and everyone who was with him. *(Fold sections B and C over section A.)*

The Lord saved Israel that day, and the Israelites saw His great works. They believed the Lord and His servant Moses.

God led His people to the Promised Land. He was with them the entire journey—a pillar of fire by night and a pillar of cloud by day—to guide His people.

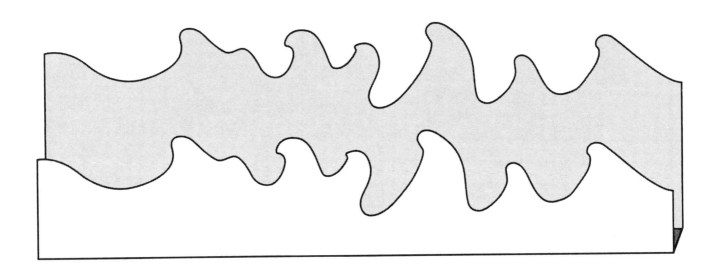

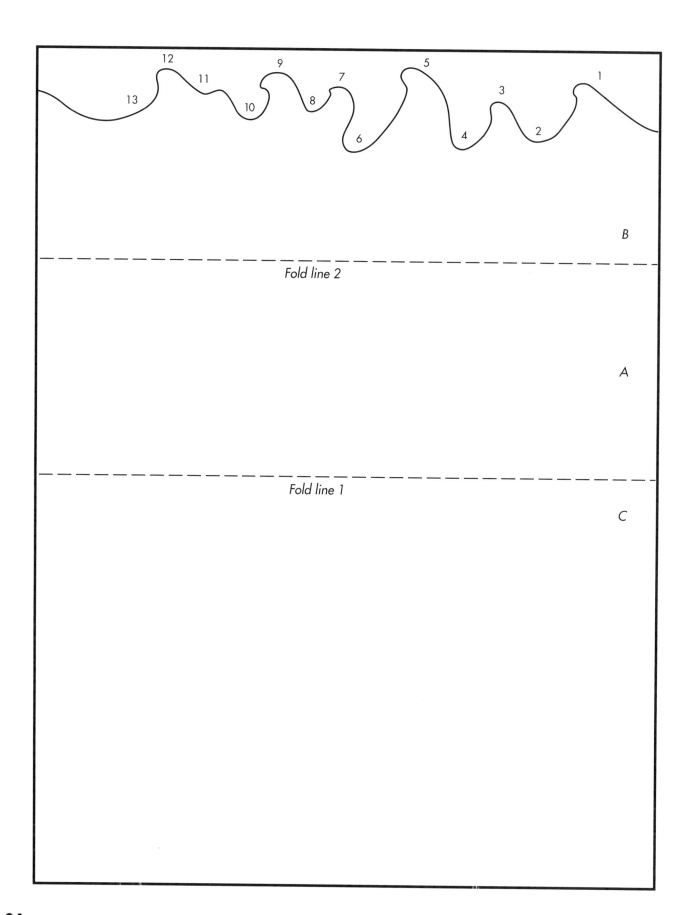

12 9 5

11

13 10 8 7 4 3 1

6 2

B

Fold line 2

A

Fold line 1

C

Samson's Riddle

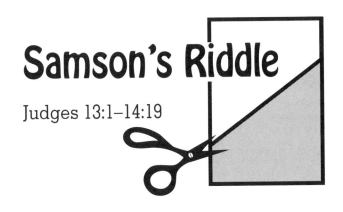

Judges 13:1–14:19

Material: One 8½ × 11 sheet of yellow paper, scissors
Preparation: None.
  For folding and cutting directions, see the pattern on page 27.

Manoah and his wife had no children. One day the angel of the Lord appeared to Manoah's wife. The angel told her that she would have a son. Then the angel told her some strange things. First, the angel said that no one should cut her son's hair. Second, the angel said that her son would free his people from the Philistines. The woman told her husband, and they both thanked God. When their son was born, Manoah and his wife named him Samson. The boy grew to be a man, and the Lord blessed him.

One day Samson went to Timnah. While he was there, he met a young woman, a daughter of a Philistine. The Philistines ruled the Israelites. When he returned home, Samson told his mother and father about the woman. "Go down and arrange for her to be my wife," Samson said to his father. *(Fold paper in half.)* Manoah did not want Samson to marry a Philistine. But Samson was sure that this was the woman he wanted to marry so he and his parents went to Timnah to talk with the woman and her family. As they walked, a young lion roared and ran at Samson. God gave Samson the strength to kill the lion with his bare hands. *(Cut 1 to 2.)*

Later, when Samson returned to Timnah for the wedding, he walked by the same spot where the lion had attacked him. Samson looked at the lion's dead body. A swarm of bees had made a nest in the body. It was full of honey. Samson scraped some of the honey out with his hands and ate it. Samson shared some of the honey with his parents, but they didn't know where he had found it. *(Cut 2 to 3.)*

After he arrived in Timnah, Samson prepared a great feast. The wedding celebration would last seven days. Thirty men from the town came to help Samson celebrate. *(Cut 3 to 4.)*

"Let me ask you a riddle," Samson said to these men. "If you can tell me the answer by the end of the celebration, I will give each of you a linen robe and a set of clothes. But if you cannot tell me the answer, then you will give me thirty linen robes and thirty sets of clothes."

"Ask your riddle," said the men.

"Here is the riddle," Samson said. "Out of the eater, something to eat; out of the strong, something sweet." *(Cut 4 to 5.)*

Three days passed, but Samson's companions had not guessed the riddle. On the fourth day, they asked Samson's wife to give them the answer to the riddle. They even threatened to burn her family's house if she didn't find out.

Samson's wife was scared. "If you love me, tell me the riddle," she begged Samson, and she began to cry.

"I haven't even told my parents," Samson said. "Why should I tell you?" *(Cut 5 to 6.)*

His wife pouted and cried during the rest of the feast. Finally, on the seventh day, Samson told his wife the answer. *(Cut 6 to 7.)* She ran and told the thirty men.

On the seventh day, just before sunset, the thirty men came to Samson. "What is sweeter than honey?" they said. "What is stronger than a lion?" *(Cut 7 to 8.)* They had answered the riddle.

"If you had not forced my wife to tell you, you would never have guessed my riddle," said Samson. *(Cut 8 to 9.)*

Samson was angry that the men had cheated to answer his riddle. *(Cut 9 to 10.)* He gave the men the robes and clothes but left Timnah and returned to his parents' house. *(Cut 10 to 11.)* Samson became a powerful judge in Israel, and God used his strength to free the Israelites from the Philistines.

Remember Samson's riddle: "Out of the eater, something to eat; out of the strong, something sweet"? In the riddle, the "eater" was a lion. The honey was the something "sweet." Honey is made by one of God's special creations—the honey bee. *(Unfold.)*

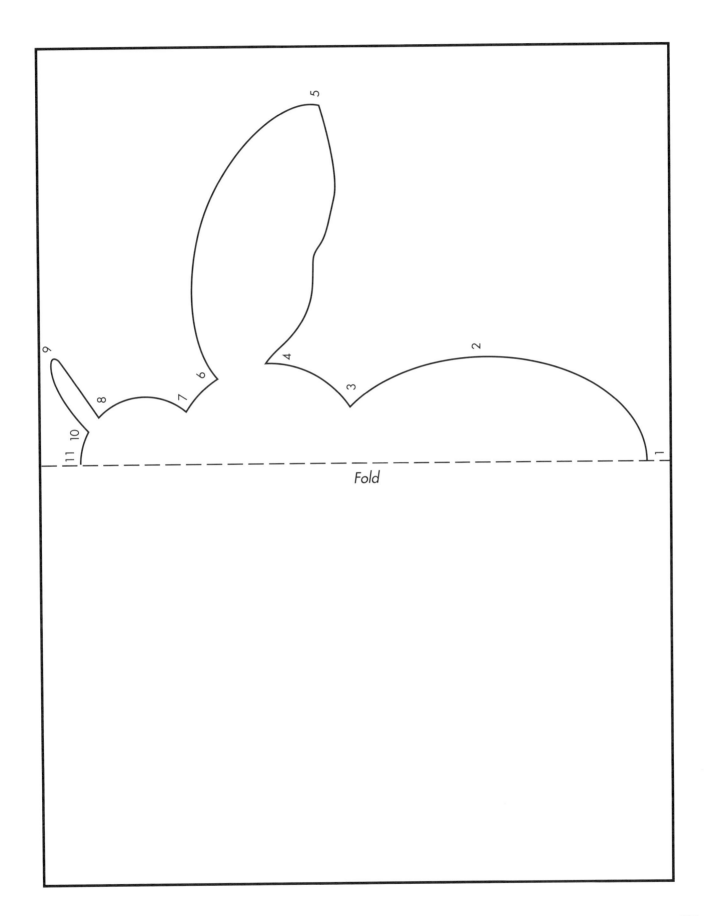

Fold

The Littlest King

2 Kings 22:1–23:28;
2 Chronicles 34:1–35:19

Materials: One 8½ × 11 sheet of paper, scissors
Preparation: None.
For folding and cutting directions, see pattern on page 29.

Many different kings ruled the Israelites. *(Fold paper in half.)* The youngest king to rule the country of Judah was Josiah. *(Cut 1 to 2.)*

Prince Josiah grew up in the palace. His father, Amon, had been king for two years. *(Cut 2 to 3.)* But Amon sinned against God and did evil. *(Cut 3 to 4.)* He worshiped idols and disobeyed God's laws. He made God angry. *(Cut 4 to 5.)*

King Amon's helpers killed him and made little Josiah king of Judah. *(Cut 5 to 6.)* Josiah did not know how to be a king. He was only eight years old. He did not know how to rule the land. *(Cut 6 to 7.)* He had to be taught about the government. He had to learn how to be a ruler. But Josiah learned his lessons and wore his *(unfold)* crown proudly.

When Josiah was 16, he learned all he could about God. Josiah was a good king and wanted to obey God. He wanted his people to obey God too. When Josiah was 20 years old, he started to change some things in his kingdom. *(Refold crown.)* He made his people stop worshiping idols. Instead, they worshiped the one true God. Josiah tore down the altars and the idols the people used to worship. *(Cut off crown point X.)*

Then Josiah called together the carpenters, the goldsmiths, and the stonecutters. "I want you to help me make God's temple beautiful again," he told them. "I want the people to come to God's house to worship Him." *(Cut off crown point Y.)*

Josiah sent his helper Shaphan to the temple. "Go to the Lord's house and see how much money has been given by the people," Josiah told Shaphan. "Give it to the men who oversee the repairs to the house of the Lord. I want it cleaned and repaired. Buy new timber, cut new stones, put in a new floor—do whatever needs to be done." *(Cut off crown point Z.)*

The temple was in ruins. Soon the workers had rebuilt the walls, doors, and floors. They washed and cleaned everything. The people worked hard to make God's house beautiful. *(Cut 8 to 9.)*

While they were cleaning, Hilkiah, the priest, told Shaphan, "I have found the Book of the Law." *(Unfold. Continue the story as you slowly roll the paper into a scroll.)* Hilkiah gave the book to Shaphan. He took the book to King Josiah.

"All the work at the temple is finished," Shaphan said. "And here is a book the priest found." *(Show rolled scroll.)* Shaphan read the book to King Josiah. When Josiah heard what Moses had written, he was sad because his people had not obeyed God's laws. Josiah sent Hilkiah and some others to visit a wise woman and learn more about the words in the book. The wise woman told Hilkiah that God was angry because the people had not obeyed Him and that He would punish them. "But tell Josiah," she said, "that because he was sorry for his sins and the sins of his people, he will be spared. God has heard his prayers." Hilkiah and his men returned to King Josiah and told him what they had learned.

Josiah ordered all the people to gather together. The priests and the prophets, all the important people, and all the common people came. They all went to the house of the Lord. Josiah, who was now 26 years old *(unroll scroll),* read the words of the book to the people. The king promised God that he would follow Him and keep His laws. The people made this promise too. As long as King Josiah lived, the people followed God.

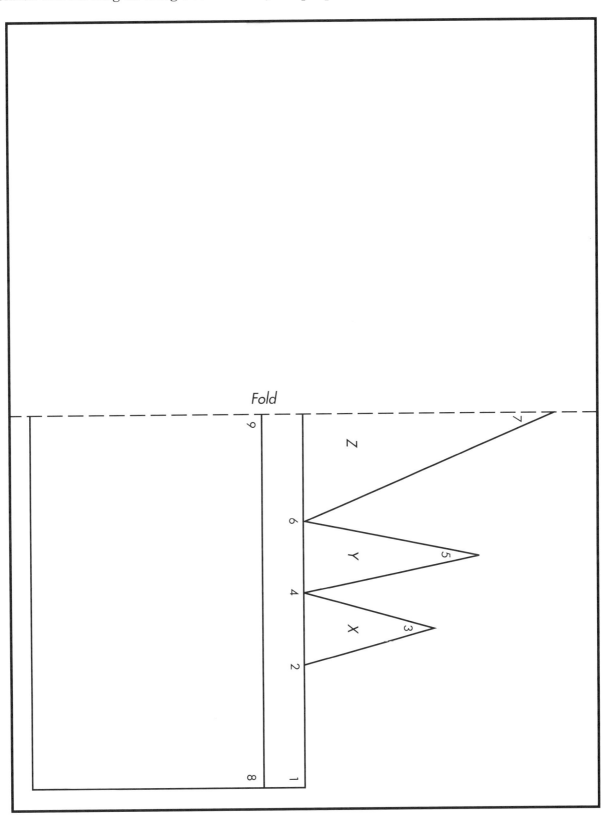

It's Cool in the Furnace

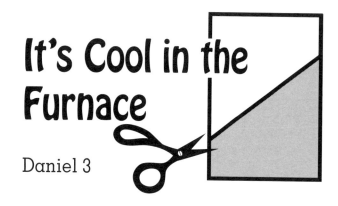

Daniel 3

Material: One 8½ × 11 sheet of white paper, scissors, broken red and yellow crayons

Preparation: Remove the paper from the crayons. Color a two-inch strip along one long edge of the paper using the flat side of the red crayon. Turn the paper over and repeat along the same edge. Color over the red with the yellow crayon to give the illusion of flames. Accordion pleat the paper to form eight 1¼" sections. For folding and cutting directions, see the pattern on page 32.

King Nebuchadnezzar ruled Babylon. He led an army that defeated the Israelites. Some of the young men were taken back to Babylon—among them Daniel and three of his friends. King Nebuchadnezzar gave these young men special training so they could help him rule Babylon.

God was with Daniel. He blessed Daniel and his friends with special talents. Daniel even helped the king to understand his dreams. The king made Daniel and his friends—Shadrach, Meshach, and Abednego—members of his court. They became King Nebuchadnezzar's advisors.

One day, Nebuchadnezzar told his workers to make an idol of gold. He put it where everyone could see it. *(Cut 1 to 2.)* Then Nebuchadnezzar sent word about the idol to all the important people. Princes, governors, captains, judges, and rulers from all around came and stood before the king's golden statue. *(Cut 2 to 3.)*

A herald read the king's orders. "The king commands all people: Whenever you hear the special music of the cornet, flute, harp, and other instruments playing together, you must fall down and worship our king's golden image. Anyone who does not obey this order will be thrown into the fiery furnace." *(Cut 3 to 4.)*

The music began. Immediately, all the people bowed down around the golden idol. All except Shadrach, Meshach, and Abednego. *(Cut 4 to 5.)*

Some people saw that they did not bow down and ran to tell the king. King Nebuchadnezzar got very angry. He ordered the three men to be brought before him. "Shadrach, Meshach, and Abednego, is it true that you did not bow down and worship my golden image?" he asked.

"Yes, it's true," the men answered. *(Don't cut 5 to 6. Cut 6 to 7.)*

"I'll give you one more chance," said the king. "When you hear the music, bow down and worship my image. If you don't, I will have you thrown into the fiery furnace. Then who will save you?"

"Our God will save us. But even if He chooses not to, we will never worship your image," said the three men. *(Cut 7 to 8.)*

Nebuchadnezzar's face became red. He got even angrier. "Heat up the furnace and make it seven times hotter than usual. Tie up these three men and throw them into the burning fire," he ordered.

The guards tied up Shadrach, Meshach, and Abednego and put them into the fiery furnace. *(Cut out shaded area.)* The fire was so hot that it killed the guards.

King Nebuchadnezzar looked into the opening at the bottom of the furnace. "Didn't you put only three men into the furnace?" he asked. *(Unfold.)*

"Yes, only three," replied his advisors.

"Look!" said the king. "I see four men, and they are no longer tied up. They are walking free and aren't hurt. One looks like a son of the gods. How could that be?"

God was with Shadrach, Meshach, and Abednego. Even in the hot, burning flames, God protected them.

King Nebuchadnezzar neared the door of the furnace. "Shadrach, Meshach, and Abednego, come here to me," he called. *(Refold. Cut 9 to 10.)*

The three men walked out of the fire. *(Unfold three men, keeping the fourth folded back.)* The flames had not touched them. Everyone looked at Shadrach, Meshach, and Abednego. Neither their clothes nor their hair was burned, and they didn't even smell of smoke.

This amazed King Nebuchadnezzar. "Blessed be the God of Shadrach, Meshach, and Abednego," the king said. "He sent His angel to keep them safe in the fiery furnace. These men loved and trusted their God. There is no other god like their God."

King Nebuchadnezzar changed his law. The people no longer had to worship the golden image that he had made. He told the people that no one would be allowed to say anything against the God of Shadrach, Meshach, and Abednego.

The king promoted Shadrach, Meshach, and Abednego. But no matter what they did, they continued to worship the one and only God.

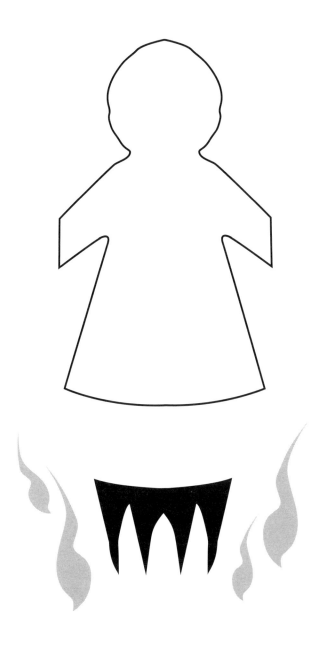

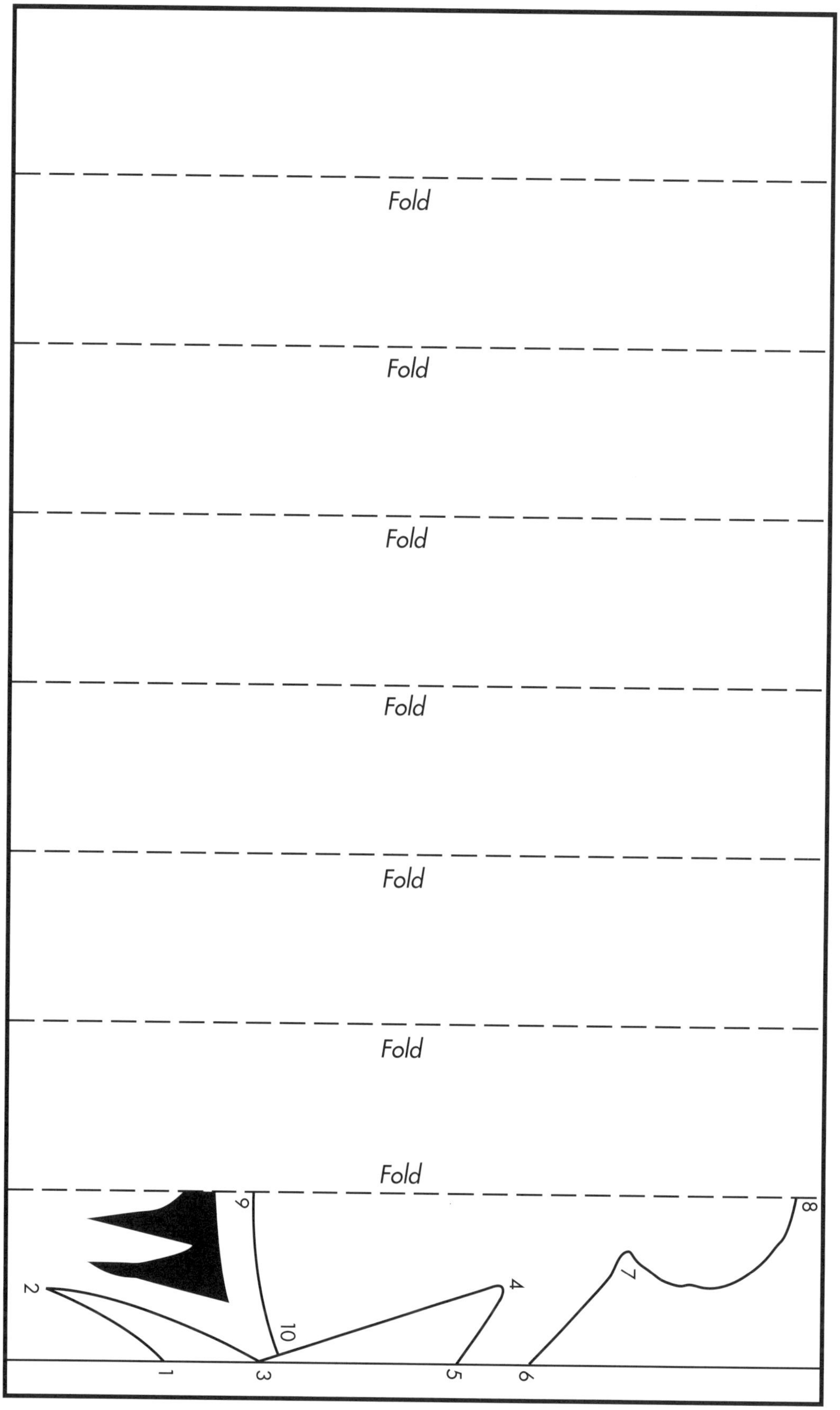

Fold

Fold

Fold

Fold

Fold

Fold

Fold

Daniel & the King

Daniel 6

Materials: One 8½ × 11 sheet of yellow paper, scissors, hole punch
Preparation: None.
   For folding and cutting directions, see pattern on page 35.

Daniel was a good man. He loved God very much. No matter what he was doing, Daniel prayed to God three times a day. Daniel worked for King Darius. The king knew that Daniel was a good man, so he placed Daniel in a high office and made him the chief over many princes and leaders. *(Fold along line A.)*

Some of the leaders who worked under Daniel did not like him. They knew the king planned to make Daniel ruler over the whole kingdom. They were jealous and wanted to find a way to get rid of Daniel. They met together to decide what to do. *(Fold along line B.)* But they couldn't find any way to make Daniel look bad because Daniel was honest and fair with everyone. What could they do?

"Let's go to King Darius," said one, "and have him make a law that everyone must pray to the king." The others liked the idea. They knew Daniel prayed to the real God and wouldn't pray to the king.

The leaders went to the king. "King Darius," said one, "you are a great and mighty king. Make a law requiring everyone

to pray only to you for the next thirty days. If they pray to any other god, have them thrown into a lions' den." *(Fold along line C.)*

King Darius liked the idea and made the law. He put the law in writing so it could not be changed.

Daniel heard about the new law, but he still prayed three times each day, giving thanks to God just as he had always done. *(Cut 1 to 2.)*

The men spied on Daniel. One day, they saw him praying to God. They ran to tell King Darius. They reminded the king that he had signed the law that said no one could pray to any god or man except to the king for thirty days. Anyone caught disobeying the law would be put into a den of lions. "King Darius," they said, "Daniel doesn't pay any attention to you or your new law. He prays three times a day to his God."

The king was sorry that he had made the law. He loved Daniel and wished he could save him. *(Cut 2 to 3.)* The king knew he could not change the law he had made.

"Throw Daniel to the lions. It's the law; you can't change it," the men yelled.

The king had Daniel brought to him. "Daniel, you broke my law, so I have to throw you into the lions' den. But I hope that your God will save you," the king said. *(Cut 3 to 4.)*

Daniel was put into the lions' den. There was no way for Daniel to climb out. And even if he could, a stone was placed over the door that opened into the pit. The king sealed the stone so no one could get to Daniel. Then King Darius went back to his palace. *(Cut 4 to 5.)*

King Darius was so worried that he could not eat or sleep. He spent all night worrying about Daniel. He got up early the next morning and ran to the lions' den. The king looked down into the den. Sadly he called down into the pit, "Daniel, Daniel, was your God whom you love and serve able to save you?" *(Cut 5 to 6.)*

"Yes, O king, and may you live forever," Daniel answered. "My God sent His angel to close the lions' mouths. They have not hurt me because I did not do anything wrong." *(Cut 6 to 7.)*

The king was so happy. "Bring Daniel up to me," he ordered. The king looked at Daniel to make sure he was all right. The king knew that because Daniel believed in God, he was not hurt by the lions. *(Punch out hole.)* Then the king ordered that the men who had spied on Daniel be thrown into the lions' den.

King Darius wrote a letter to all the people of the land. *(Cut 8 to 9.)* "Daniel's God is the true and living God," he wrote, "and all people should fear and love Him. His kingdom will not be destroyed, and He will rule forever. He does great things in heaven and on earth. He will keep His people who love Him from harm, just like He protected Daniel from the lions." *(Unfold to reveal lions.)*

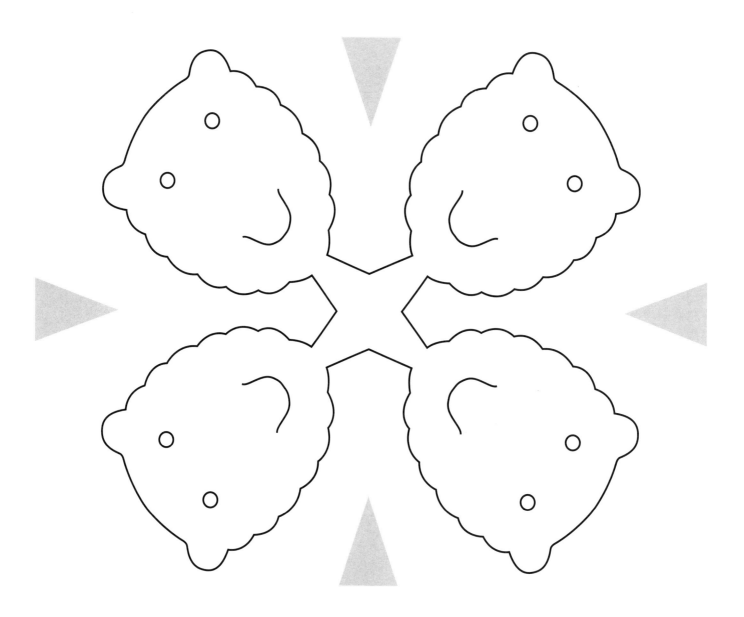

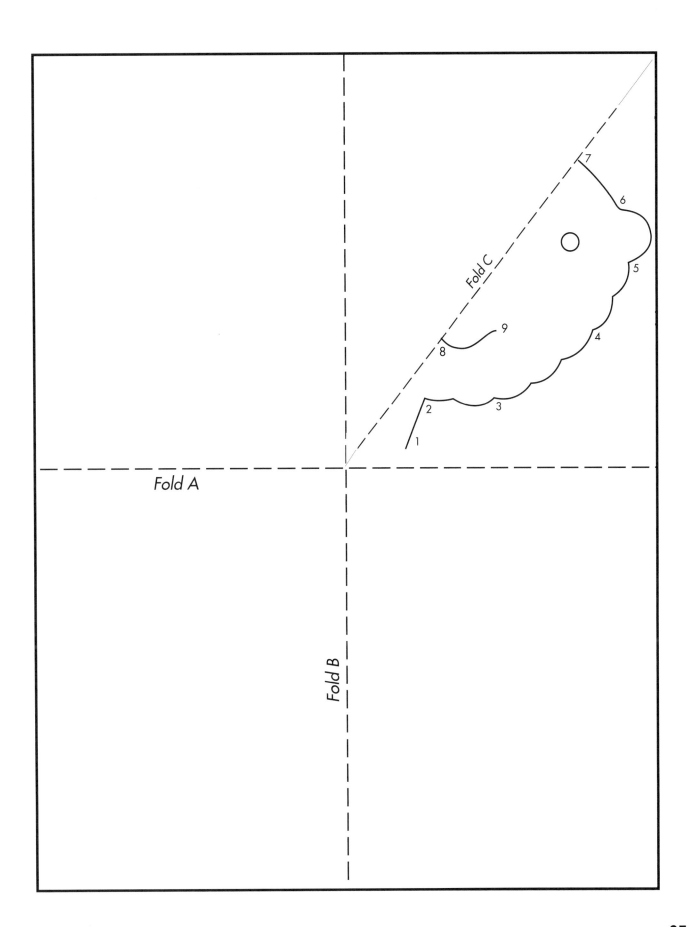

Fold C

Fold A

Fold B

7

6

5

4

3

2

1

9

8

Jonah's Ride

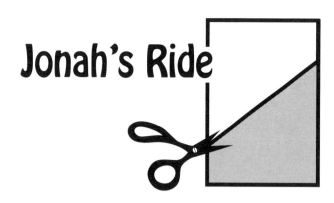

The Book of Jonah

Materials: One 8½ × 11 sheet of light gray paper, scissors
Preparation: None.
For folding and cutting directions, see the pattern on page 38.

One day, God talked to a man named Jonah. *(Fold paper lengthwise.)* "Jonah, go to the city of Nineveh," God said. "The people there are sinful. I want you to tell them about Me and about My laws. Go, now." *(Cut 1 to 2.)*

Nineveh was the capital of Assyria, a country at war with Jonah's country. Jonah did not want to go to Nineveh, so he ran away in the opposite direction. *(Cut 2 to 3.)*

Jonah tried to hide from God. He went to the city of Joppa and found a ship that was sailing to Tarshish, a city far away. Jonah paid his fare and boarded the ship. He thought God would not find him there. *(Cut 3 to 4.)*

But God knew where Jonah was. He sent a great wind that stirred up the sea. The wind turned into a mighty storm. The huge waves nearly covered the ship as the wind tossed it around. The storm was so bad that the sailors were afraid the ship would be broken in half. Everyone prayed to their god for help.

"Throw things overboard to lighten the ship so it won't sink," said the sailors. *(Cut 4 to 5.)* They tossed everything they could over the side of the ship.

Jonah did not hear the storm. He was sleeping below the deck of the ship. The captain woke him and said, "Why are you sleeping? Get up and pray to your God to save us. If you don't, we're going to drown!" *(Cut 5 to 6.)*

The sailors were very scared. They asked Jonah who he was, what country he was from, and why he was on their ship. Jonah told them he was a Hebrew and that he worshiped the one true God. He also told them he was trying to run away from God.

"What can we do so the wind and the storm will stop," the sailors asked Jonah. *(Cut 6 to 7.)*

"Throw me into the sea," Jonah said, "and then the sea will be calm again."

The sailors did not want to throw Jonah into the sea. They tried other things instead. The men rowed hard and tried to bring the boat to land, but they could not. *(Cut 7 to 8.)* The storm just grew stronger and stronger. Finally, the sailors looked at Jonah, and they looked at the high waves coming into the boat. They realized there was nothing else to try. They took Jonah and threw him into the sea. Immediately, the sea became calm. *(Cut 8 to 9.)*

God knew what happened to Jonah. He told a giant fish to swim to Jonah. *(Unfold.)* The fish opened its mouth and swallowed Jonah. *(Refold. Cut 9 to 10. Unfold.)* Jonah was safe inside the fish's stomach. He stayed there for three days and three nights. It must have been dark and wet inside the fish.

Jonah prayed while he was in the fish. Jonah told God that he was sorry for disobeying Him. Jonah thanked God for saving him. He promised to follow God and do everything that God wanted.

God loved Jonah and heard his prayer. After three days God told the fish to swim to dry land. Then the fish opened its mouth wide *(refold; cut line A; unfold)* and spit Jonah out. Then it swam away. *(Remove the fish.)*

Jonah found himself on a beach. What a surprise it must have been. Jonah had not been hurt inside the giant fish because God had taken care of him. Again God said, "Jonah, go to Nineveh and preach."

Jonah walked for three days until he came to the city of Nineveh. He told the people about God. He said that in forty days God would destroy Nineveh because everyone in the city had done sinful things.

The news reached the king. He told his people to pray to God and to turn from their sinful ways and follow the one true God. The people listened to Jonah and the king and did what God wanted them to do.

God saw that they were sorry and that they wanted to follow Him. He did not destroy Nineveh. God saved the people of that city.

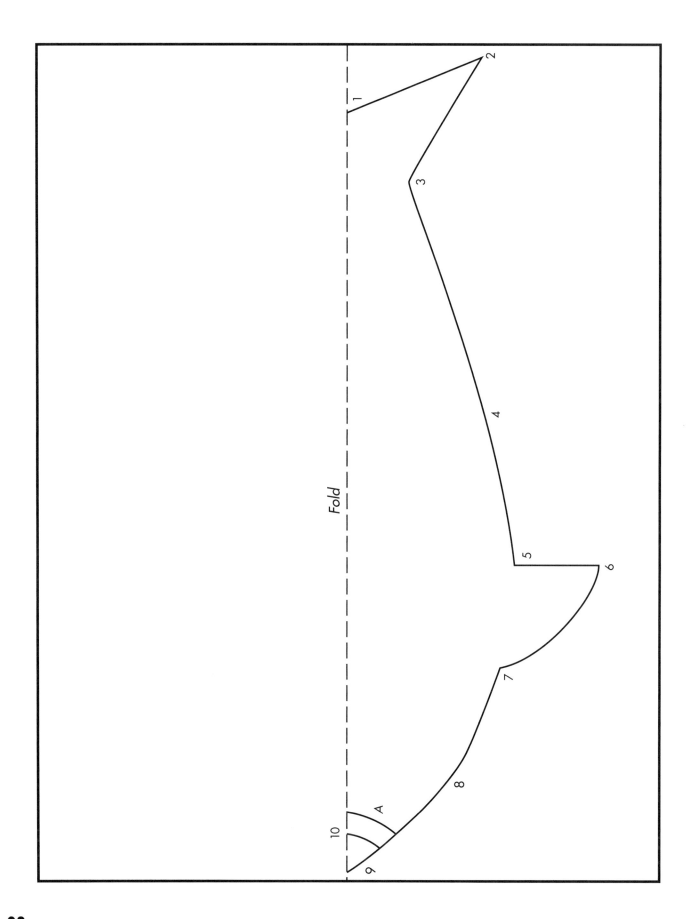

Fold

1
2
3
4
5
6
7
8
9
10
A

38

New Testament

God's Messengers

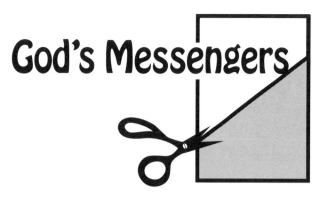

Miscellaneous passages

**Materials: One 8½ × 11 sheet of
white paper, scissors
Preparation: None.
For folding and cutting directions, see the pattern on page 42.**

Angels are mentioned in the Bible often. They appear in both the Old and New Testament. Angels speak, disappear, reappear, are dressed in white, and seem to have a bright light shining around them. Many of the people who saw angels were afraid of them. *(Fold paper lengthwise.)*

Angels never preached; they only brought messages from God. We don't know a lot about angels, but we do know that they were God's special messengers.

(Slowly cut line A as you tell this story from Luke 1:5–25.)

One day, when a man named Zechariah was in the temple, one of God's messengers suddenly appeared by the altar. Zechariah was afraid.

"Don't be afraid, Zechariah, your prayer has been heard," said the messenger. "Your wife, Elizabeth, will have a son. You will name him John. He will bring joy and happiness to you and your wife. He will be a great man, and he will work for the Lord."

Zechariah didn't believe God's messenger. He asked for some proof. The messenger told Zechariah that he wouldn't be able to speak until the baby was born. When Zechariah left the temple, he couldn't talk!

Elizabeth did have a baby. When Zechariah named the child John, he was able to speak again, just as the messenger had said. When John grew up, he prepared the people for the coming of Jesus. John baptized many people, including Jesus.

God's messenger to Zechariah was an *(unfold)* angel. *(Refold.)*

(Slowly cut line B as you tell this story from Luke 1:26–38.)

God sent His messenger Gabriel to take a message to Mary. Mary was alone when she saw the messenger. She did not know who it was.

"Don't be afraid, Mary," said Gabriel. "You have been chosen by God. You will have a baby and will name Him Jesus. He will be the Son of God. He will be a great person, and He will save His people."

"I don't understand," Mary said. "I am not even married yet. How can this be?"

"God has a plan," the messenger answered. "Nothing is impossible for Him."

It happened just the way the messenger said. Mary had a baby, and she named Him Jesus. When He grew up, He died and rose again to save His people.

God's messenger to Mary was an *(unfold)* angel. *(Refold.)*

(Slowly cut line C as you tell this story from Matthew 1:18–25.)

God sent a messenger to take a message to Joseph. Joseph was a good man. He was honest and fair and loved God. Joseph had been thinking about Mary and the preparations for their wedding. God's messenger came to him in a dream.

"Don't worry, Joseph," the messenger said. "God loves you and everything will be all right. Go ahead with your plans for the

wedding. Mary will have a Son by the power of the Holy Spirit. You will name the baby Jesus."

Joseph did as the messenger said. He married Mary.

God's messenger to Joseph was an *(unfold)* angel. *(Refold.)*

(Slowly cut line D as you tell this story from Luke 2:8–20.)

God used one of His messengers to announce an important event to the world. The messenger did not bring this important news to kings or princes but to some lowly shepherds. These shepherds had the night watch in a field near Bethlehem. They were protecting the sleeping sheep from wild animals.

The shepherds may have been walking around, quietly checking on the sheep, or perhaps they were resting. Suddenly, the messenger appeared. The shepherds were surprised and frightened to see the messenger. "Don't be afraid," the messenger said. "God sent me to bring you good news.

"Today in the town of David a Savior has been born to you; He is Christ the Lord. Go to Bethlehem and you will find God's Son lying in a manger."

The messenger that brought the good news to the shepherds was an *(unfold)* angel. *(Refold.)*

(Slowly cut line E as you tell this story from Matthew 28:5–7.)

Jesus grew up. He traveled the country, healing the sick and preaching. He talked to the people and told them about God.

After three years of teaching, Jesus' enemies had Him arrested. They sentenced Jesus to death. Jesus died on the cross to pay the price for our sins and was buried in a tomb. Early on a Sunday morning, some women went to the tomb. A messenger was waiting for them.

"Don't be afraid," said the messenger. "I know you are looking for Jesus, but He is not here. He has risen from the dead. Go and tell His disciples."

The messenger at the tomb was an *(unfold)* angel.

Many times the Bible tells us that God sent angels as His messengers.

(Unfold and show each cutout as you review the angelic visits.)

An angel told Zechariah that his son, John, would be born.

An angel told Mary that she would have Jesus, God's Son.

An angel told Joseph about Mary's baby.

An angel told the shepherds that Jesus was born.

An angel told the women at the tomb that Jesus was alive.

Angels really are God's special messengers!

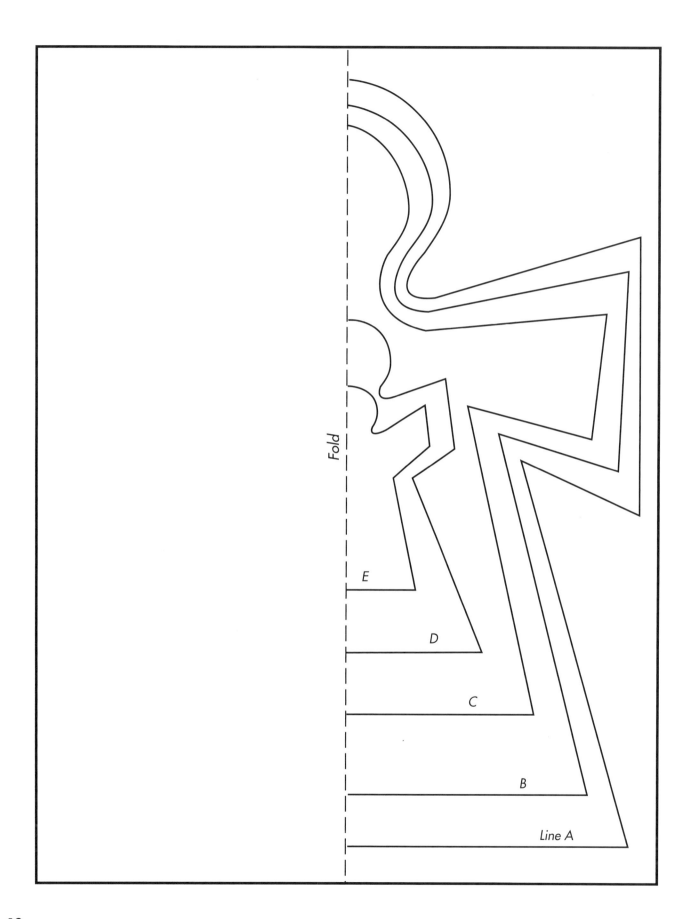

Fold

E

D

C

B

Line A

42

The First Christmas

Luke 2:1–20;
Matthew 2:1–23

Materials: One 8½ × 11 sheet of yellow paper, scissors
Preparation: None.
For folding and cutting directions, see the pattern on page 44.

Christmas is the day we celebrate Jesus' birth on earth. He grew up to be our Savior. *(Fold along line A.)*

Joseph and Mary were living in Nazareth. Soon they would be married. *(Fold along line B.)* An angel had visited both Joseph and Mary and told them that Mary would have a baby. They were to name the baby Jesus. Jesus would be a special baby because He was God's Son.

The ruler of the country where Joseph and Mary lived sent out an important order. *(Cut 1 to 2.)* All the people had to return to the towns where they were born to sign their names to a book. Then the king would know how many people he had in his kingdom. *(Cut 2 to 3.)*

"We need to go to Bethlehem," Joseph told Mary.

Mary packed her things. Joseph loaded the donkey. Joseph walked, leading the donkey. *(Cut 3 to 4.)* Mary rode on the donkey because she was going to have her baby soon.

The trip was long. It took Joseph and Mary several days to reach Bethlehem. *(Cut 4 to 5.)* When they arrived in the town, so many people were there that Joseph could not find a place to stay. There were no big hotels or motels, just little inns where a few people could spend the night and get something to eat. *(Cut 5 to 6.)*

When Joseph asked for a room, one innkeeper said, "There is no room here, but there is a stable where you can stay." *(Cut 6 to 7.)*

Joseph and Mary went to the stable. It had been a long trip, and Mary was tired. *(Cut 7 to 8.)* That night Jesus was born in the stable. Mary wrapped Him in a long piece of soft cloth. Joseph took a manger that was used for feeding the animals and filled it with clean, soft hay. It would be the baby's cradle. Mary laid the baby in the manger. *(Cut 8 to 9.)*

Not far away, some shepherds were guarding their sheep. An angel appeared to them and said, "Don't be afraid. I have some news that you will be happy to hear. Tonight, in Bethlehem, the Savior, Christ the Lord, was born. *(Cut 9 to 10.)* You will find Him lying in a manger." Suddenly, many angels filled the sky. They praised God, saying, "Glory to God in the highest and on earth, peace among men." *(Cut 10 to 11.)*

The shepherds talked about the things they had heard. *(Cut 11 to 12.)* "Let's go right now and see this baby that God's angel has told us about," they said. *(Cut 12 to 13 and unfold.)*

The shepherds hurried as fast as they could to Bethlehem. *(Refold. Cut 14 to 15.)* They searched and searched and finally found the baby lying in a manger, just like the angel had said. *(Unfold and set stable upright.)* The shepherds were the first to hear the good news, and they were the first to visit the family. When they left the stable, they told everyone they saw about the good news of the Savior.

Jesus was God's Christmas gift for the whole world.

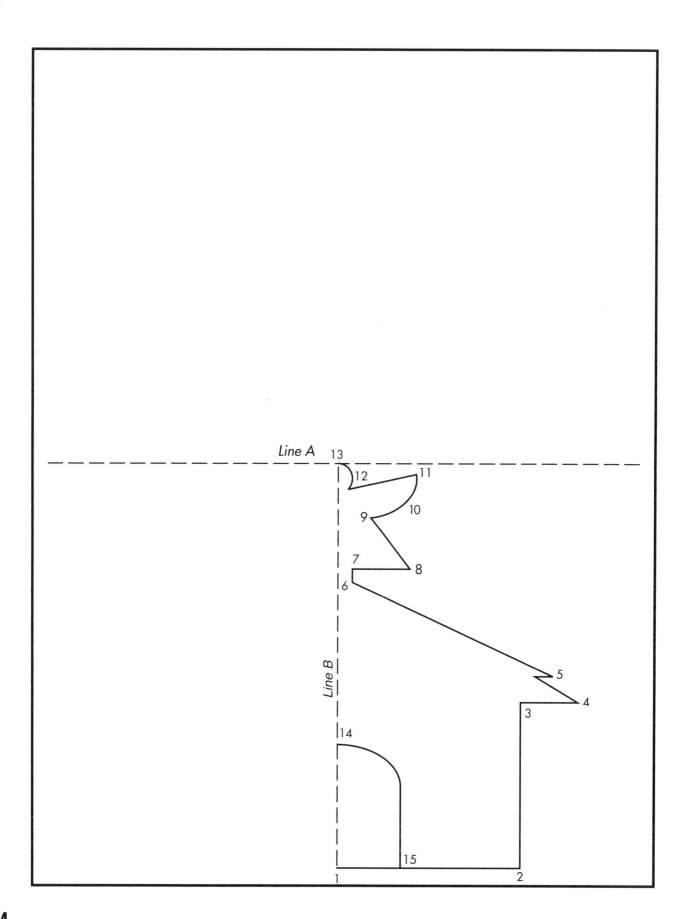

Line A

Line B

Jairus' Daughter

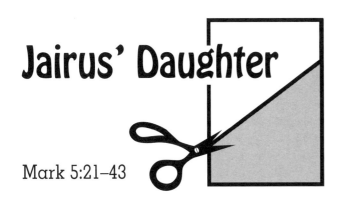

Mark 5:21–43

Materials: One 8½ × 11 sheet of paper, scissors
Preparation: None.
For folding and cutting directions, see the pattern on page 46.

One day, Jesus and His disciples sailed across the Sea of Galilee. By the time they reached the other side, a big crowd of people had gathered to hear Jesus speak.

In the crowd was a man named Jairus. He was a ruler of the synagogue. While Jesus was speaking, Jairus ran to Jesus and fell down at His feet. *(Fold along line A.)*

"Jesus," he said, "my little girl is dying. Please come and lay Your hands on her so she will be healed." Jairus had only one daughter and he loved her very much. She was about 12 years old. *(Cut 1 to 2.)*

Jesus went with Jairus. His disciples followed Him. Many people joined them until a big group of people crowded around Jesus as He walked. *(Cut 2 to 3.)*

A woman who had a disease that no doctor could cure came up behind Jesus. She had spent all her money, but the doctors had been unable to make her well. "If I can just touch the edge of Jesus' robe," she said to herself, "I will be healed." She reached out and touched the hem of Jesus' robe. Immediately, she knew she was healed. She felt well again. *(Cut 3 to 4.)*

"Who touched My clothes?" Jesus asked. *(Cut 4 to 5.)*

"There are so many people crowding around us that it could have been anyone," the disciples said.

Jesus looked around and found the woman who had touched His robe. The woman was afraid. Trembling, she fell down before Jesus and said, "I touched Your robe." *(Cut 5 to 6.)*

"Daughter, your faith has made you well," Jesus said. "Go in peace, and be free from your suffering." *(Cut 6 to 7.)*

Before Jesus finished talking to the woman, some people came from Jairus' house and told Jairus, "Your daughter is dead."

Jesus told Jairus not to be afraid, but to believe. Then Jesus continued on His way with Jairus. Only Peter, James, and John were allowed to come with them.

When the group neared Jairus' house, people rushed out of the house, crying. *(Cut 7 to 8.)*

"Why are you so upset? Why are you crying?" Jesus asked. "She is not dead, only asleep." *(Cut 8 to 9.)*

The people laughed at Jesus because they knew she was dead.

Jesus took the girl's mother and Jairus and His disciples and went into the little girl's room. He walked toward the bed. *(Unfold, creasing line B back.)* "Little girl," He said, "I say to you, arise." *(Refold to original A fold.)*

The little girl opened her eyes. *(Cut 10 to 11.)* Jesus took her by the hand and she stood up. *(Crease line C forward so figure stands up.)*

The little girl went to her parents. She was walking! "Give her something to eat," Jesus said.

Everyone was surprised to see that the little girl was alive. Jesus told Jairus and his wife not to tell anyone about what had happened. But people all over the land heard about this wonderful thing that Jesus had done for the daughter of Jairus. It was a miracle.

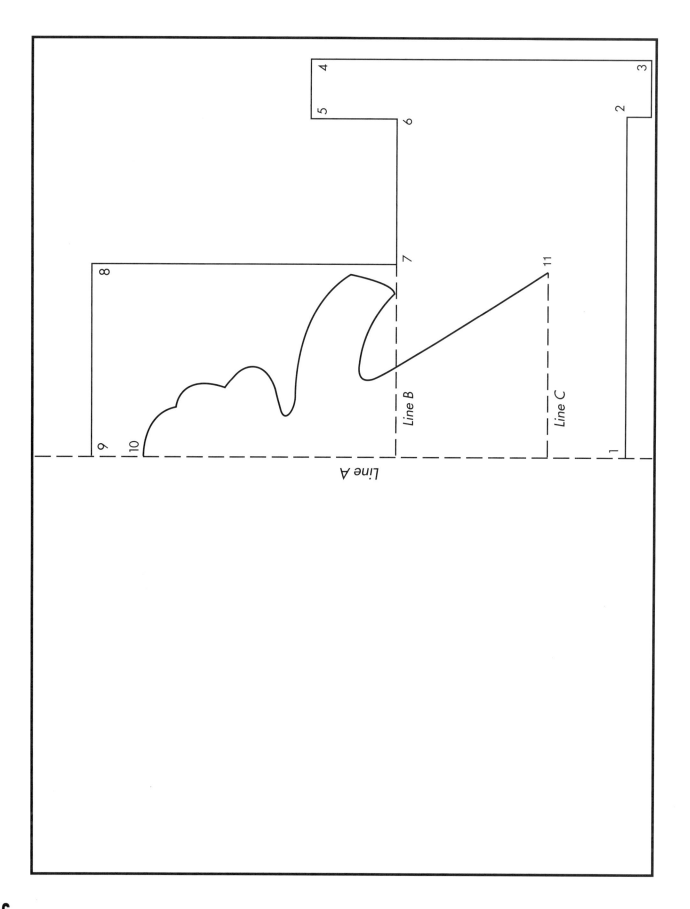

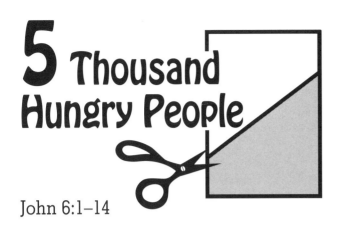

5 Thousand Hungry People

John 6:1–14

Materials: One 8½ × 11 sheet of light brown paper, scissors, a black felt-tip pen
Preparation: None.
   For folding and cutting directions, see the pattern on page 48.

This is the story of a miracle. It is only one of Jesus' miracles, but God told us about it in all four gospels—Matthew, Mark, Luke, and John. *(Fold paper in half.)*

Jesus had been teaching and healing the sick. He left the crowd of people and went down by the sea. Many, many people knew Him. They left the city and ran after Him. Jesus got into a boat and sailed across the Sea of Galilee. When He stepped out of the boat, a large crowd of people was waiting for Him. *(Cut 1 to 2.)*

Jesus spoke to the people about God's love and His kingdom. He taught them many things. All day the men, women, and children sat and listened. They must have loved to hear Jesus talk and teach them. *(Cut 2 to 3.)*

When it was getting late in the day, the disciples said to Jesus, "This is a desert. There is nothing to eat here. Send all these people away so they can buy food and find a place to spend the night." *(Cut 3 to 4.)*

"They don't need to leave," Jesus answered. "They can eat here. You give them food." *(Don't cut 4 to 5. Cut 5 to 6.)*

"We don't have any fo said. "And we don't have buy even a little bit of fo *(Cut 6 to 7.)*

"How much food asked. *(Cut 7 to 8.)*

Andrew, one of His disciples, answe "A boy in the crowd has five loaves of barley bread and two small fish. But it is not enough for the thousands of people that are here." *(Cut 8 to 9.)* How could so little food ever be enough for all those people?

"Bring the boy's lunch to Me," said Jesus. "Tell the people to sit down." The disciples did as Jesus told them. The people sat in the grass, just like it was a giant picnic. *(Cut 9 to 10 to 11.)* Then the disciples brought the boy's lunch to Jesus. *(Unfold.)*

When everyone was seated, Jesus took the fish and the bread in His hands. Jesus looked up toward heaven and blessed the bread and broke it. He did the same with the fish. Then Jesus handed the bread and fish to His disciples. They passed it out to all the people, and everyone ate as much as they wanted. About five thousand men, plus women and children, ate that meal. The little boy must have been surprised to see how Jesus fed all the people with his lunch.

When everyone had finished eating, Jesus told His disciples to gather up the leftovers. The disciples went through the large crowd with baskets. They gathered enough leftovers to fill *(draw a large 12 on the basket)* twelve baskets with the pieces of bread and fish.

When the people saw the miracle that Jesus had performed, they said, "This is surely the true Savior." They wanted to make Jesus their king, but Jesus wouldn't let them. He told His disciples to get into their boat and row to Bethsaida, a city on the other side of the sea. Then Jesus walked away from the place where He had fed the people. He climbed a mountain to be alone and to pray.

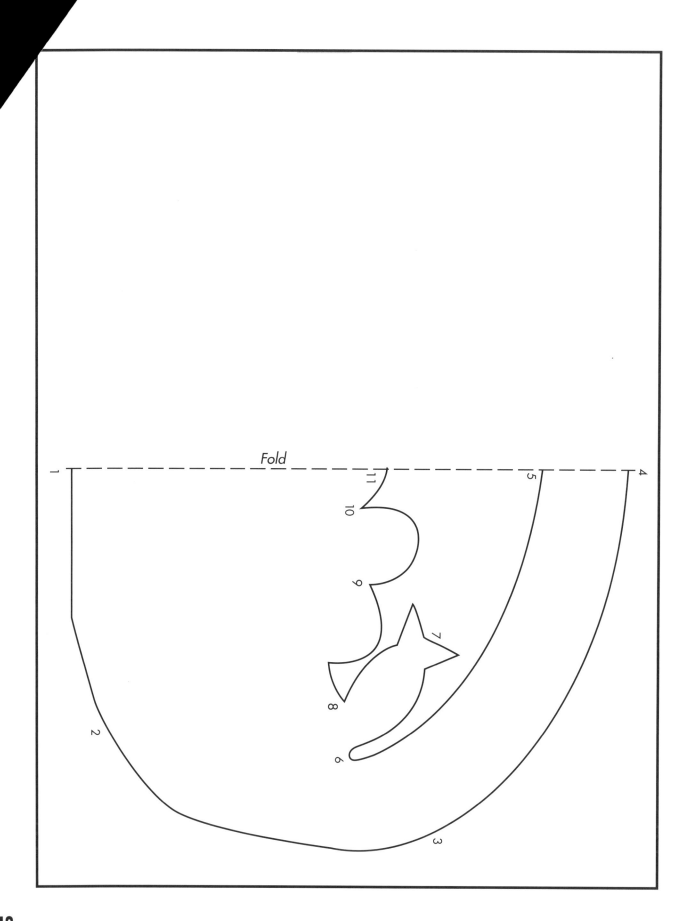

Fold

The Good Neighbor

Luke 10:25–37

Materials: One 8½ × 11 sheet of brown or gray paper, scissors
Preparation: None.
For folding and cutting directions, see pattern on page 50.

One day, Jesus was speaking to His disciples and a large crowd of people who had come to hear Him teach. In the crowd was a lawyer. "What must I do to have eternal life?" the lawyer asked. *(Fold paper in half.)*

"You have read the law," Jesus answered. "What does it say?" *(Cut 1 to 2.)*

The man looked surprised. He was trying to trick Jesus to see if He really was the Son of God. *(Cut 2 to 3.)* "Well," said the man, "the law says to love the Lord your God with all your heart, with all your soul, with all your strength, with all your mind; and to love your neighbor as much as you love yourself." *(Cut 3 to 4.)*

"That is right," said Jesus, "and if you do this, you will live with God forever." *(Cut 4 to 5.)*

Still testing Jesus, the lawyer asked, "If I am supposed to love my neighbor, then tell me, who is my neighbor?" *(Cut 5 to 6.)*

Jesus replied with a parable, or a story, to help the lawyer and the crowd better understand His answer. This is the parable Jesus told to the crowd.

"A man was traveling from Jerusalem to Jericho. He was walking alone on the steep, hilly road. Some thieves waiting by the side of the road saw the man. They jumped out at him, beat him, tore his clothes, and took his money. The thieves left the man lying beside the road, wounded and almost dead. *(Cut 6 to 7.)*

"A priest, walking down the same road, saw the man but didn't bother to stop. He crossed over and went down the other side of the road. The priest hurried on his way. *(Cut 7 to 8.)*

"A second man, a Levite, came along the road. He saw the man lying in the dust, but he quickly crossed the road also and went down the other side. *(Cut 8 to 9.)*

"Soon a third man, a Samaritan, came by. He saw the poor man lying by the side of the road. The Samaritan jumped off his donkey and began to help the man. Carefully, the Samaritan washed and bandaged the man's wounds. Then he gently lifted the man onto his donkey. The Samaritan walked as he led the donkey to a nearby inn. The Samaritan took care of the injured man. *(Cut 9 to 10.)*

"The next day the Samaritan had to leave, but he said to the innkeeper, 'Here is some money. Take care of this man for me. After I finish my business, I will be back. If I owe you any more money, I will pay you then.' The innkeeper agreed to take care of the injured man. The Samaritan continued on his journey." *(Cut 10 to 11.)*

Jesus looked at the lawyer. "Which of these three men proved to be a neighbor to the wounded man?" Jesus asked. "Was it the priest, the Levite, or the Samaritan?" *(Cut 11 to 12. Conceal cutout.)*

"It was the man who stopped and helped the man who was hurt," said the lawyer.

Yes, it was the man who stopped to help and took the man on his *(stand up cutout)* donkey to the inn. The Samaritan showed that he was a good neighbor. Jesus told the lawyer to go and do as the good neighbor had done.

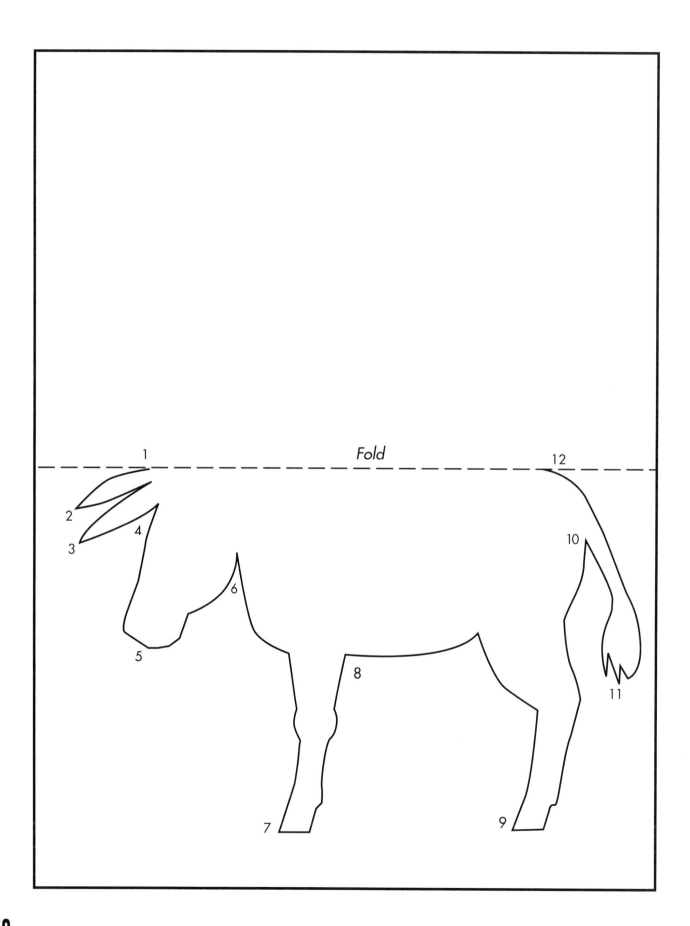

Fold

The Little Man with the Big Heart

Luke 19:1–10

Materials: One 8½ × 11 sheet of green paper, scissors
Preparation: None.
    For folding and cutting directions, see the pattern on page 53.

Jesus had been traveling around the country healing the sick, teaching His disciples, and preaching. As He entered the town of Jericho, He stopped to heal a blind beggar who was sitting by the roadside. *(Fold paper lengthwise.)* Then He passed on through the town. *(Cut 1 to 2.)*

Wait! Who's the little man pushing his way through the crowd, running back and forth, jumping up and down, trying to see Jesus? It's Zacchaeus, trying hard to see over the heads of all the people in the crowd. *(Cut 2 to 3.)*

Zacchaeus was a rich man. He was in charge of a large office of tax collectors. Tax collectors went around to all the homes and businesses and made the people pay the government the amount of money that they were told to pay. Tax collectors where known for collecting more money than they were supposed to collect. Then they kept the extra money for themselves. The people did not like Zacchaeus, so he didn't have many friends. *(Cut 3 to 4.)*

Zacchaeus had heard about Jesus, especially that He was friends with tax collectors. Could Jesus like me too? he wondered. Zacchaeus wanted to find out. He had heard that Jesus was coming to his town, and he saw many people moving slowly down the street and crowding around someone. This must be Jesus, he thought. *(Cut 4 to 5.)* But Zacchaeus could not see whom it was. He could not see over the heads of the people. Zacchaeus was afraid he might not get to see Jesus.

When he saw the crowd coming his way, Zacchaeus ran ahead and climbed up in a tall sycamore tree. The little man crawled out on a limb, leaned down, and waited for Jesus to pass. Now he would be sure to see Jesus. *(Cut 5 to 6.)*

Jesus and the crowd of people moved slowly down the street. Zacchaeus waited. Jesus stopped by the tree. He looked up at the little man and said, "Zacchaeus, hurry and climb down from that *(unfold)* tree. It's important that I go to your house today."

Quickly Zacchaeus crawled back on the limb and slid down the trunk of the tree. He brushed off his clothes and smiled up at Jesus. He was very happy. *(Refold.)* Jesus went home with Zacchaeus. *(Cut 7 to 8.)*

The people were surprised. "Why would Jesus want to stay at the house of someone like Zacchaeus?" they asked one another. *(Cut 8 to 9.)* "He's a rich tax collector and a sinner." *(Cut 9 to 10.)* They didn't understand that Jesus had come to save people like Zacchaeus.

Jesus talked with Zacchaeus. *(Cut 10 to 11.)* Zacchaeus listened closely because he knew that Jesus loved everyone, even tax collectors. *(Cut out X.)*

"Lord, I know I have sinned, and I'm sorry," Zacchaeus said. "I've taken money that wasn't mine. I'm going to give half of everything I have to the poor and needy. If I've lied to anyone or taken what I shouldn't, I'm going to give it back. In fact, I'll give back four times what I took." *(Cut out Y.)*

Jesus said, "Zacchaeus, this day salvation has come to your house, for the Son of Man came to find and to save the lost."

Zacchaeus knew that Jesus was the Son of God. He knew that Jesus had come to look for sinners and to save them. How happy Zacchaeus was. The little man, who climbed up in a tree so he would be able to see Jesus, said good-bye to his Savior. Jesus went on His way.

If you come across a big tree, stop! *(Unfold the tree cutout.)* Think of the little man with the big heart who entertained Jesus in his house. *(Unfold the house cutout.)*

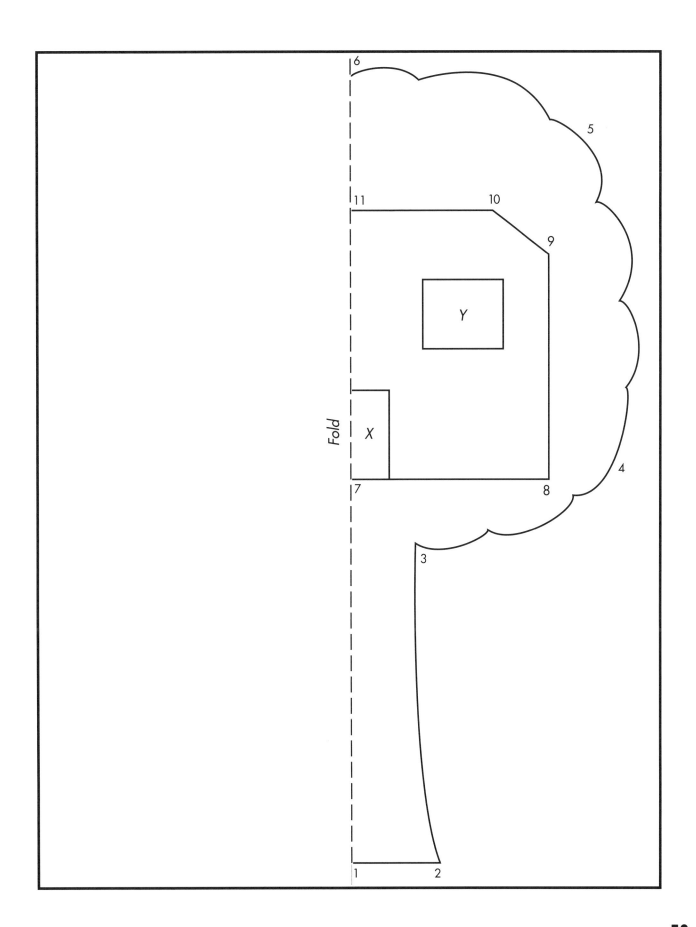

Fold

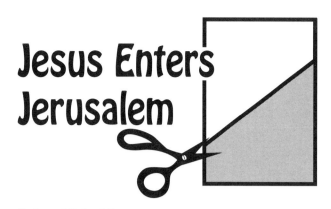

Jesus Enters Jerusalem

John 12:1–15;
Matthew 21:1–11

**Materials: One 8½ × 11 sheet of light
green paper, scissors**
Preparation: None.
  **For folding and cutting direc-
  tions, see the pattern on page 55.**

Six days before the Passover, Jesus and His disciples traveled to Bethany to visit Lazarus. *(Fold paper lengthwise.)* Lazarus' sisters, Mary and Martha, lived there too. *(Cut 1 to 2 to 3.)* Mary and Martha fixed a meal. Martha served the guests. Lazarus sat at the table with Jesus and the disciples. *(Cut 3 to 4.)*

Mary came into the room with a jar of sweet smelling, very expensive perfumed ointment. *(Cut 4 to 5.)* She poured it on Jesus' feet, then wiped His feet with her long hair. The room was filled with the sweet smell of perfume. Mary did this because she loved Jesus. This perfume was the best thing she had to give Him. *(Cut 5 to 6.)*

Judas, one of the disciples, asked, "Why did Mary do that? She could have sold the perfume and given the money to the poor." *(Cut 6 to 7.)* Judas did not really care about helping the poor. He was a thief and wanted to put the money into the money bag, which he carried.

"It is all right for Mary to do this good thing," Jesus answered. "You can help the poor every day; there always will be poor people who need you. But I will not be here

long because I am going to heaven soon to be with My Father." *(Cut 7 to 8.)* This, then, was the best time for Mary to do something special for Jesus.

Jesus and His disciples left to go to Jerusalem. "Go into the village," Jesus said to two of His disciples. "There you will find a donkey and her colt. Untie them and bring them back to Me. If anyone asks what you are doing, just tell them that the Lord needs them." *(Cut 8 to 9.)* This happened because long ago it had been said that the King would ride into Jerusalem on a donkey.

The disciples went into the village. They found the donkey and her colt. They untied the animals and brought them back to Jesus, just as He had told them to do. *(Cut 9 to 10.)*

The disciples took off their coats and laid them on the donkey. Then they put Jesus on the donkey. A crowd of people began to gather. Some of the people took off their coats and covered the path leading into Jerusalem. *(Cut 10 to 11.)* Others cut branches from palm trees and laid them on the road. *(Cut 11 to 12.)*

Some people went ahead of Jesus and His disciples; others followed behind. People from Jerusalem came out to meet Jesus. *(Cut 12 to 13 to 14.)* They were waving *(unfold)* palm branches. *(Wave the palm frond.)* It was like a parade. The people shouted and sang, "Hosanna to the Son of David! Blessed is He that comes in the name of the Lord."

We remember that day when people waved palm branches as Jesus rode into Jerusalem. We call it Palm Sunday.

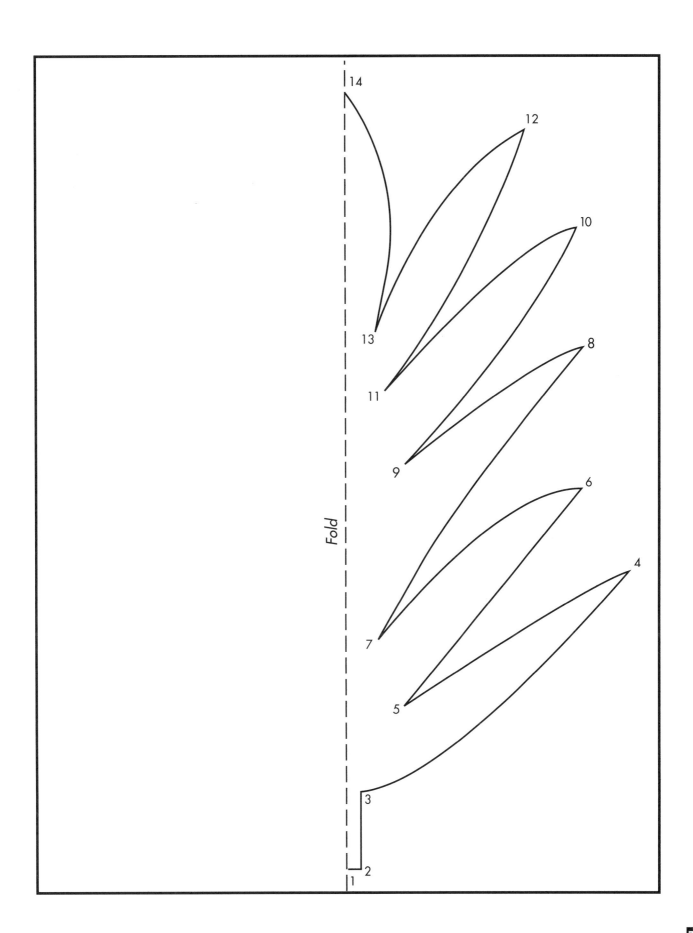

Fold

He Is Risen!

Matthew 27:57–66; 28:1–8;
Mark 15:42–47; 16:1–8;
John 19:38–42; 20:1–18

Materials: **One 8½ × 11 sheet of white paper, scissors, a gray crayon or gray paint**
Preparation: **Color or paint one side of the paper gray.**
For folding and cutting directions, see the pattern on page 58.

God had promised Adam and Eve that He would send a Savior. God kept His promise when Jesus was born on the first Christmas. But God's plan to save us from our sins meant Jesus would have to die. Jesus had traveled to Jerusalem to fulfill that part of God's plan.

Jesus celebrated a special meal with His disciples, then He went to a garden to pray. There in the garden, Jesus was arrested, even though He'd done nothing wrong. After several trials, Jesus was sentenced to die. The Roman soldiers nailed Jesus to a cross. He died for the sins of all people.

After Jesus died, Joseph, a man from Arimathea, *(fold paper in half with gray side out)* asked Pilate, the Roman ruler, for Jesus' body. He wanted to bury it. Pilate gave Joseph permission to take the body. *(Cut 1 to 2.)*

Joseph took Jesus' body down from the cross and wrapped it in a clean, linen cloth. *(Cut 2 to 3.)* He placed the wrapped body in a tomb that had been carved out of a large rock in a garden near where Jesus had died. *(Cut 3 to 4.)* Joseph rolled a heavy stone in front of the opening to the tomb. *(Cut 4 to 5. Unfold.)* Then Joseph went home. Mary Magdalene and another Mary saw where Joseph placed Jesus' body.

Jesus' enemies went to Pilate and said, "Jesus said that after three days He would rise again. Do something or His disciples will steal His body and say that He is alive again."

Pilate ordered that the stone should be sealed and that guards should watch the tomb day and night. All of this happened on Friday. *(Refold.)*

Early on the first day of the week, Sunday, just as the sun was rising, a group of women went to the tomb to anoint Jesus' body with spices. *(Cut 6 to 7.)* On their way, the women wondered who would roll away the stone from the door. *(Cut 7 to 8.)* When they arrived, the stone already had been rolled away! *(Cut 8 to 9.)* Mary Magdalene saw Jesus' empty tomb *(cut 9 to 10 to 11)* and ran to tell Peter and John.

The other women walked toward the tomb. *(Cut 11 to 12.)* They saw the *(unfold, showing white side of cutout)* angel who had rolled back the heavy stone. The angel, dressed in a long robe that was as white as snow, sat on the stone. The women were frightened.

"Don't be afraid," the angel said. "I know that you are looking for Jesus who was crucified. He is not here; He is risen just as He said He would. Come and see the place where the Lord lay."

The women looked in the empty tomb. "Go and tell the disciples that Jesus has risen and that He is going to Galilee," said the angel. "He will meet them there just as He promised." *(Refold.)*

The women ran quickly from the tomb. Meanwhile Mary Magdalene told Peter and John about the empty tomb. *(Cut 13 to 14.)* They ran to the garden to see for themselves. Mary followed them. *(Cut 14 to 15.)* Peter and John went into the tomb. *(Cut 15 to 16. Unfold, showing gray side of paper.)* They saw the clothes placed neatly on the place where Jesus' body had been. The two men left.

Mary remained alone at the tomb, crying. She stooped down and looked into the tomb. She saw two angels, one at the head and one at the foot of the place where Jesus' body had been.

"Woman, why are you weeping?" they asked.

Mary answered, "Because they have taken away my Lord, and I don't know where they have put Him."

As she turned around, she saw someone standing near her. He said, "Why are you crying? Who are you looking for?" the man asked.

Mary thought it must be the gardener. "If you know where they have put Him, tell me and I will take Him away."

But it was not the gardener; it was Jesus. "Mary," He said.

She turned and said to Him, "Rabboni," which means teacher.

"Go and tell the others that I am going to go up to heaven to My Father and your Father, to My God and your God," Jesus said.

Mary went and told the disciples all that Jesus had said. "I have seen the Lord," she said.

After that Jesus appeared to many others before He ascended into heaven. Jesus didn't need the *(show angel)* angels to help Him out of the tomb; His resurrection was part of God's plan too. But He sent the angels to take His message to Mary and the women. Then these women and His disciples shared the message of Jesus' resurrection with the whole world.

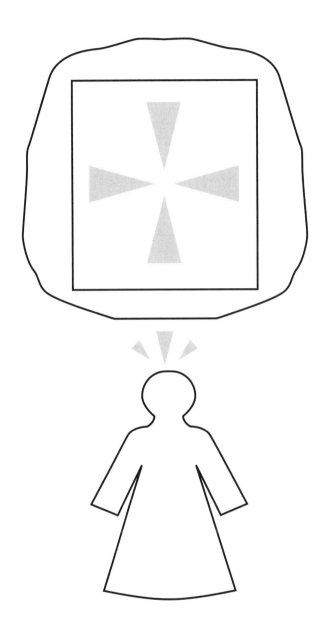

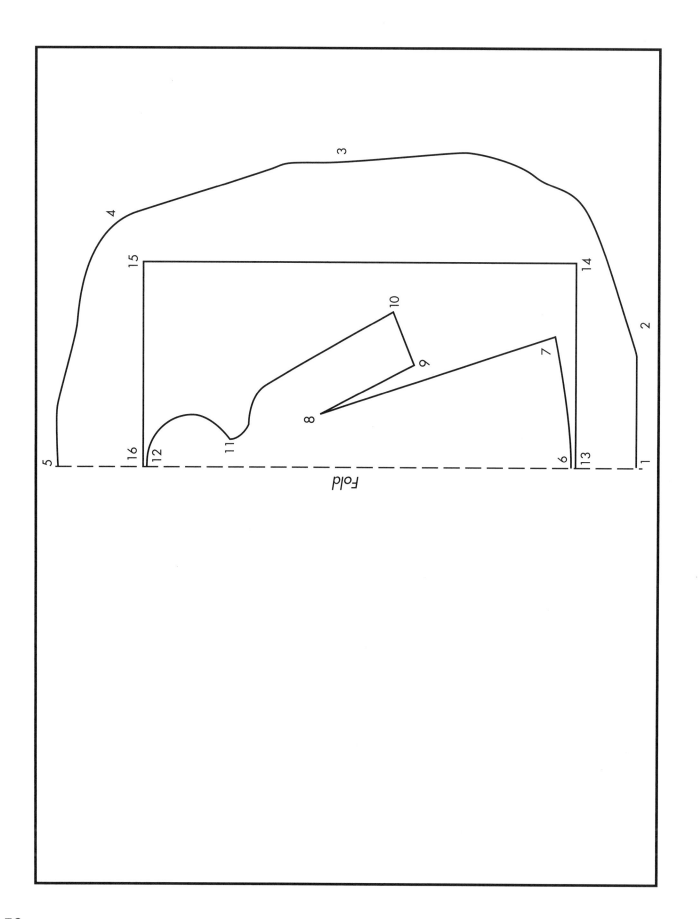

Let Down Your Nets

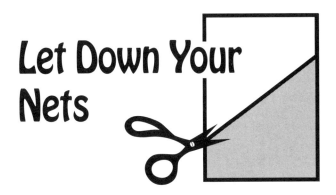

John 21:2-12

Materials: **One 8½ × 11 piece of brown or yellow paper, scissors**
Preparation: **Accordion pleat the paper into eight 1″ sections. For folding and cutting directions, see the pattern on page 60. Fill a clear container with 153 small items—wooden beads, counters, or small plastic fish.**

After the resurrection, the disciples returned to Galilee as Jesus had told them to do. They waited for Him to come and tell them what to do next. *(Cut 1 to 2 to 3.)*

While they waited, they kept busy doing their old job—fishing. *(Cut 3 to 4.)* Many people in Bible times were fishermen. They fished all day and even into the night. Sometimes they caught many fish; other times they did not catch any. They ate some of the fish and traded some for other things they needed.

Peter, Thomas, Nathanael, James, John, and two other disciples were mending their fishing nets. As they worked on the nets, Peter said, "I'm going fishing."

"We'll go with you," the others said. *(Don't cut 4 to 5. Cut 5 to 6.)*

Everyone climbed into the boat and rowed out onto the water. They threw out their nets and waited. The men fished all night, but they did not catch any fish. *(Cut 6 to 7 to 8 to 9.)*

The next morning, Jesus stood on shore waiting. The disciples saw a man, but they did not know it was Jesus. *(Cut 9 to 10.)* "Have you caught any fish?" Jesus called out.

"No," they answered.

"Pull up your nets and throw them down on the right side of the boat," Jesus said. "Then you will find fish." *(Don't cut 10 to 11. Cut 11 to 12.)*

Quickly the men pulled up the nets and moved them to the right side of the boat. Into the water went the nets. When the disciples started to pull up the nets, they were so heavy with fish that the men couldn't get the nets in the boat. *(Cut 12 to 13 to 14 to 15.)*

The disciples rowed the boat to shore, dragging the heavy net behind them. *(Cut 15 to 16.)* On shore, they saw a fire with fish and bread cooking on it. "Bring some of the fish that you caught," Jesus said. *(Don't cut 16 to 17. Cut 17 to 18.)*

Peter pulled on the net full of fish. They had caught 153 fish, but the net was not broken. *(Slowly unfold as you tell the rest of the story. First show three fish, then six, nine, and 12 fish.)* "Come and eat," Jesus said, and He served His friends bread and fish.

(Have the children help you count the fish in the cutout, then tell them there were many more fish in the disciples' nets. Show the container filled with 153 items. Explain that if each item were a fish, this would be the number of fish the disciples caught in their nets.)

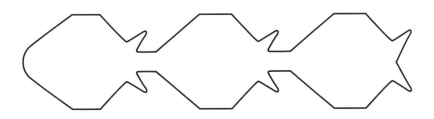

1
2
3
4
5
6
7
8
9
10
11
12
13
14
15
16
17
18
Fold
Fold
Fold
Fold
Fold
Fold
Fold

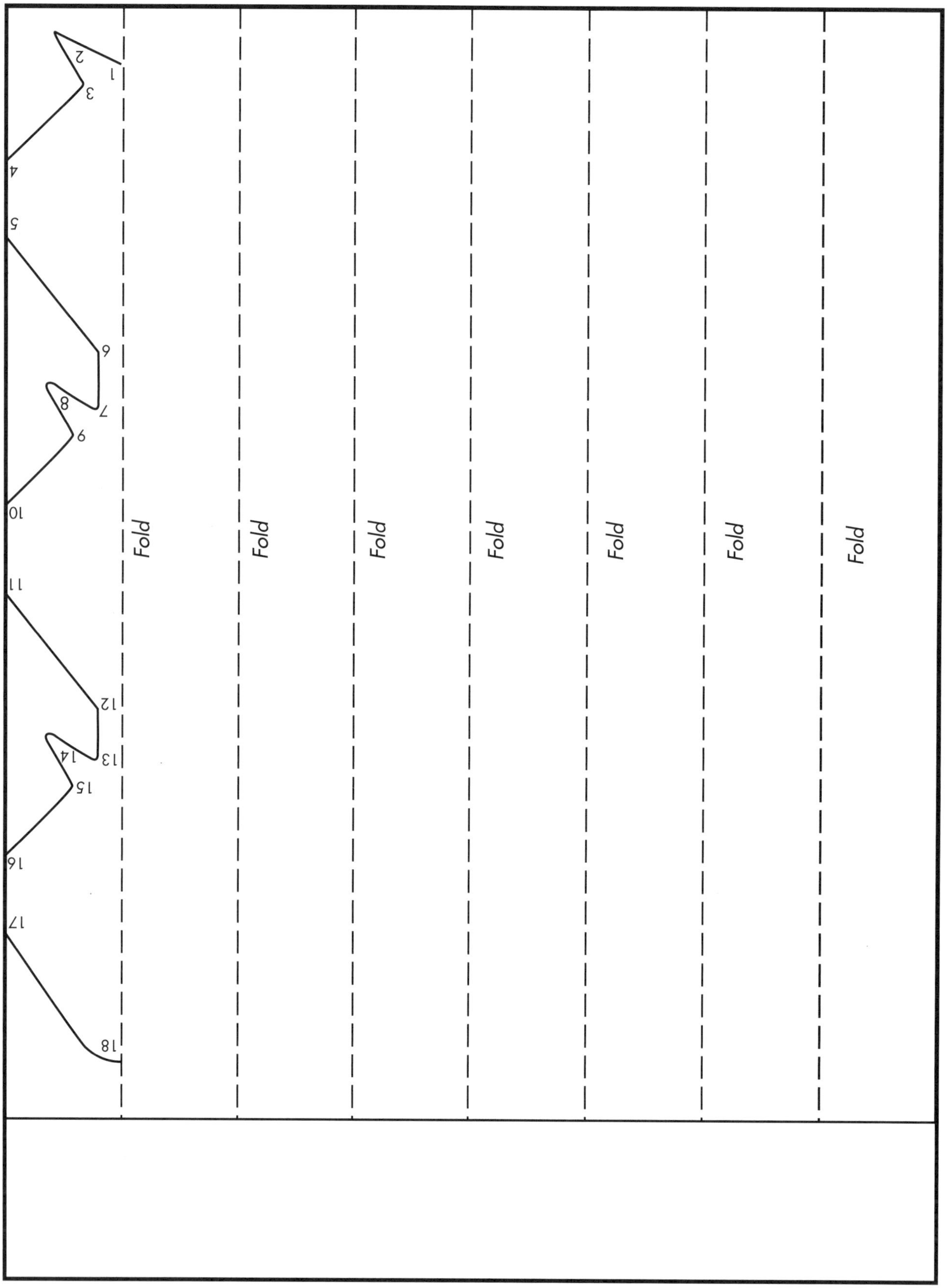

Dorcas' Special Talent

Acts 9:36–42

Materials: One 4¼ × 11 sheet of colorful paper (or wallpaper), scissors

Preparation: Accordion pleat the paper into six 1½″ sections. For folding and cutting directions, see the pattern on page 62.

A special woman lived in the city of Joppa. Her Hebrew name was Tabitha, but she usually was called by her Greek name, Dorcas. *(Cut 1 to 2.)*

Dorcas was a caring, loving woman. She helped the poor and needy. How did she do this? Dorcas could sew! No one in Bible times had a sewing machine. Instead, people used needle and thread to sew everything by hand. Dorcas used her hands to serve God, and she used her home for her workshop. *(Don't cut 2 to 3. Cut 3 to 4.)* Dorcas went to the market and bought cloth. Then she would lay it out on a table and cut out the cloth to make a shirt or a robe.

Many women of her day could sew, so why was Dorcas special? She loved Jesus with all her heart, and she wanted to serve Him and others. She shared the special talent God had given her by sewing clothing for people who didn't have any. She sewed for God. *(Cut 4 to 5.)*

Dorcas probably made tiny clothing for little babies, robes and cloaks for mothers and fathers, and clothing to keep older people warm. Everyone likes new clothes, so Dorcas made many people happy with her sewing. She probably sewed as she listened to the widows share their problems with her. The women were lonely, and Dorcas was their friend. *(Cut 5 to 6.)*

One day Dorcas became sick and died. *(Don't cut 6 to 7. Cut 7 to 8.)* Her friends were sad because they loved her. They carried her to an upstairs room. "We must do something," someone said.

"Go get Peter," another person answered. *(Cut 8 to 9.)*

Peter, one of Jesus' disciples, was preaching nearby. Two men went to get him. Peter had heard of the good things Dorcas had done for others, and he knew she loved the Lord. He went with the men to Dorcas' house. The women took him up to the room were Dorcas' body lay. *(Cut 9 to 10.)* "We miss Dorcas," the women said. "See the clothes she made for us and our children?" *(Unfold.)*

"Leave the room," Peter said. Peter knelt beside the bed and prayed. Then he turned to the body and said, "Tabitha, rise." *(Refold.)*

Dorcas opened her eyes. When she saw Peter, she sat up. He stretched out his hand, and she took it. Peter helped her to stand up. He called the women. "Here is your friend Dorcas! She is alive!"

"Dorcas is alive again," the people said. "She was raised from the dead. It's God's miracle." *(Cut line A.)* The people were so happy. They knew that this same God who loved and healed Dorcas also loved them.

The Bible doesn't tell us any more about Dorcas. But she probably continued making clothes *(unfold again)* and telling people about Jesus. Dorcas used her special talent to help others.

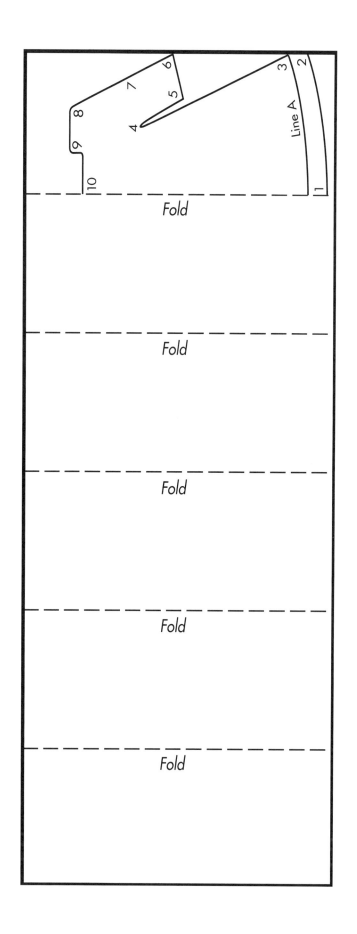

Fold

Fold

Fold

Fold

Fold